Second Language Learning and Teaching

Series Editor

Mirosław Pawlak, Faculty of Pedagogy and Fine Arts, Adam Mickiewicz University, Kalisz, Poland

The series brings together volumes dealing with different aspects of learning and teaching second and foreign languages. The titles included are both monographs and edited collections focusing on a variety of topics ranging from the processes underlying second language acquisition, through various aspects of language learning in instructed and non-instructed settings, to different facets of the teaching process, including syllabus choice, materials design, classroom practices and evaluation. The publications reflect state-of-the-art developments in those areas, they adopt a wide range of theoretical perspectives and follow diverse research paradigms. The intended audience are all those who are interested in naturalistic and classroom second language acquisition, including researchers, methodologists, curriculum and materials designers, teachers and undergraduate and graduate students undertaking empirical investigations of how second languages are learnt and taught.

Ali Derakhshan · Farzaneh Shakki

Instructed Second Language Pragmatics for The Speech Acts of Request, Apology, and Refusal: A Meta-Analysis

Ali Derakhshan
Department of English Language
and Literature, Faculty of Humanities
and Social Sciences
Golestan University
Gorgan, Iran

Farzaneh Shakki
Department of English Language
and Literature, Faculty of Humanities
and Social Sciences
Golestan University
Gorgan, Iran

ISSN 2193-7648   ISSN 2193-7656 (electronic)
Second Language Learning and Teaching
ISBN 978-3-031-37092-2   ISBN 978-3-031-37093-9 (eBook)
https://doi.org/10.1007/978-3-031-37093-9

© The Editor(s) (if applicable) and The Author(s), under exclusive license to Springer Nature Switzerland AG 2023

This work is subject to copyright. All rights are solely and exclusively licensed by the Publisher, whether the whole or part of the material is concerned, specifically the rights of translation, reprinting, reuse of illustrations, recitation, broadcasting, reproduction on microfilms or in any other physical way, and transmission or information storage and retrieval, electronic adaptation, computer software, or by similar or dissimilar methodology now known or hereafter developed.
The use of general descriptive names, registered names, trademarks, service marks, etc. in this publication does not imply, even in the absence of a specific statement, that such names are exempt from the relevant protective laws and regulations and therefore free for general use.
The publisher, the authors, and the editors are safe to assume that the advice and information in this book are believed to be true and accurate at the date of publication. Neither the publisher nor the authors or the editors give a warranty, expressed or implied, with respect to the material contained herein or for any errors or omissions that may have been made. The publisher remains neutral with regard to jurisdictional claims in published maps and institutional affiliations.

This Springer imprint is published by the registered company Springer Nature Switzerland AG
The registered company address is: Gewerbestrasse 11, 6330 Cham, Switzerland

Preface

Learning a second language (L2) requires more than mere vocabulary and structural acquisition; acquiring the principles of language use, sociocultural conventions, what to say, how to say it, how to convey meanings, and how to avoid misunderstandings are also among the crucial factors that represent how competent a speaker is in L2. Expertise in using suitable vocabulary, ensuring correct grammatical structure, and selecting pragmatically comprehensible sentences are prerequisites for successful communication. The field of L2 pragmatics is a well-grounded branch of knowledge in which these pivotal areas are addressed. Second Language Acquisition (SLA) and pragmatics are two inextricable concepts that define the objectives in L2 pragmatics. The first, SLA, deals with the experimental methods and frameworks used to scrutinize the process of learning and teaching additional languages, and the latter, pragmatics, is considered a goal for L2 acquisition in different contexts, perhaps even in various degrees (Taguchi, 2019).

Pragmatics examines the connection between context and linguistic forms, which are bound by many factors, like the topic of the conversation, the setting, the role of the interlocutors, and their relationships. Since we are responsible for the consequences our linguistic behaviors may have on others' reactions and perceptions, the significance of pragmatics is brought to the fore. Considering the complexity of learning pragmatics, achieving full competency in L2 pragmatics is almost unimaginable due to variables that may hinder the language teaching and learning process. One way to alleviate this complexity is the instruction of social norms and communication conventions in which some appropriate levels of politeness and formality are used (Taguchi, 2015). Instruction can ameliorate the variations that exist even in a single community and diminish the challenges learners may face in pragmatics learning.

L2 pragmatic instruction helps learners obtain appropriate contextual resources and use them in real interactions. For instance, when L2 learners want to convey a request to someone else, they must know the available linguistic forms, how to express their request, to whom the request will be asked, and the outcomes this request may have. Some of the prerequisites of successful communications can be provided by L2 pragmatics instruction; hence, this area of research has received much attention during the last three decades (Alcón-Soler & Martínez-Flor, 2008;

Bardovi-Harlig, 2022; Barron, 2016; Cohen & Ishihara, 2013; Derakhshan & Eslami, 2015, 2020; Félix-Brasdefer, 2008; González-Lloret & Ortega, 2018; Shakki et al, 2023; Takahashi, 2015; Taguchi, 2019; van Compernolle, 2014).

In brief, L2 pragmatics is a branch of SLA in which the pragmatic norms and the process of acquiring pragmalinguistic and sociopragmatic features are investigated so that they can be taught for better L2 performance. Meta-analyses aimed to determine if this instruction is effective and to find the variables which moderate this effectiveness are continually being conducted by researchers (Cooper et al., 2019; Oswald & Plonsky, 2010). Meta-analyses combine and aggregate the statistics of findings from previous and primary research. Researchers then use the results of multiple studies to draw appropriate inferences on their basis. Many scientific areas like psychology, education, medicine, and economics have conducted meta-analyses over the last three decades. A review of previous meta-analyses carried out on the effectiveness of L2 pragmatic instruction has revealed that, to the best of our knowledge, there has been no meta-analysis conducted on the effectiveness of the speech acts of request, apology, and refusal; instead, the literature shows a focus on specific contexts or limited inclusion and exclusion criteria that hinder the generalizability of the results.

Instructed Second Language Pragmatics for The Speech Acts of Request, Apology, and Refusal: A Meta-Analysis illustrates the long-lasting relationship between instruction and language learning, especially in the domain of L2 pragmatics. Its overview of empirical findings proves that instruction can pave the way and simplify the hardships of learning pragmatics. This book aims to represent the theoretical evidence of L2 pragmatic instruction and the visualization of the analyses based on a large corpus of studies on the instruction of request, apology, and refusal. Structurally, this book consists of six chapters. Chapter One takes into consideration the theoretical underpinnings of pragmatics, like models of communicative competence, cognitive approaches, and the noticing hypothesis. Additionally, the book's key concepts, namely pragmatics, speech acts, instructed second language acquisition, and meta-analysis, are concisely discussed. Chapter Two theoretically and empirically investigates the primary studies on the three selected speech acts. Further, the previous meta-analyses related to the topic are analyzed and reported in detail. Chapter Three presents the methodology of conducting the meta-analysis of the three aforementioned speech acts. More specifically, this chapter outlines the inclusion and exclusion criteria, the calculation of the effect sizes, the coding of the moderator variables, the missing data, the reliability of the data, and the publication bias. The penultimate chapter focuses on the results of this study in which the overall effectiveness of L2 pragmatic instruction and the variables moderating this effectiveness are presented. Chapter Five presents and compares the results of this meta-analysis study with those of the previous meta-analyses. Finally, Chapter Six deals with the conclusion, limitations, implications, and directions for further research.

We believe this monograph will be thought-provoking for researchers interested in conducting meta-analysis in L2 pragmatics. The recommendations provided in our book will open new avenues for future studies on the instruction of speech acts. In addition, other coding protocols and the inclusion and exclusion criteria may help future researchers conduct in-depth studies.

Gorgan, Iran

Ali Derakhshan

Farzaneh Shakki

References

Alcón-Soler, E. & Martínez-Flor, A. (Eds.). (2008). *Investigating pragmatics in foreign language learning, teaching and testing*. Multilingual Matters.

Bardovi-Harlig, K. (2022). Pragmatics: Speaking as a pragmalinguistic resource. *The Routledge Handbook of Second Language Acquisition and Speaking*, 243–257.

Barron, A. (2016). Developing pragmatic competence using EFL textbooks: Focus on requests. *Literacy Information and Computer Education Journal (LICEJ), 7*, 2172–2179.

Cohen, A. D. & Ishihara, N. (2013). Pragmatics. In B. Tomlinson (Ed.), *Applied linguistics and materials development* (pp. 113–126). Bloomsbury.

Derakhshan, A., & Eslami, Z. (2015). The effect of consciousness-raising instruction on the comprehension of apology & request. *TESL-EJ, 18*(4). http://www.tesl-ej.org/wordpress/issues/volume18/ej72/ej72a6/

Derakhshan, A., & Eslami Rasekh, Z. (2020). The effect of metapragmatic awareness, interactive translation, and discussion through video-enhanced input on EFL learners' comprehension of implicature. *Applied Research on English Language, 9*(1), 25–52. https://doi.org/10.22108/are.2019.118062.1476

Félix-Brasdefer, J. C. (2008). Teaching pragmatics in the classroom: Instruction of mitigation in Spanish as a foreign language. *Hispania, 91*, 479–494.

González-Lloret, M., & Ortega, L. (2018). Pragmatics, tasks, and technology: A synergy. In N. Taguchi & Y. Kim (Eds.), *Task based approaches to teaching and assessing pragmatics* (pp. 191–216). John Benjamins.

Shakki, F., Neaini, J., Mazandarani, O., & Derakhshan, A. (2023). A meta-analysis on the instructed second language pragmatics for the speech acts of apology, request, and refusal in an Iranian EFL context. *Language Related Research, 13*(6), 461–510.

Takahashi, S. (2015). The effects of learner profiles on pragmalinguistic awareness and learning. *System, 48*, 48–61.

Taguchi, N. (2015). Instructed pragmatics at a glance: Where instructional studies were, are, and should be going. *Language Teaching, 48*(1), 1–50.

Taguchi, N. (Ed.). (2019). *The Routledge handbook of second language acquisition and pragmatics*. Routledge.

van Compernolle, R. A. (2014). *Sociocultural theory and L2 instructional pragmatics*. Multilingual Matters.

Contents

1 **Overview of the Theoretical Frameworks** 1
   1.1 Introduction 1
   1.2 Instructed Second Language Acquisition 4
   1.3 Models of Communicative Competence and Pragmatics 5
   1.4 Defining Pragmatics and Interlanguage Pragmatics 5
   1.5 Cognitive Approaches in L2 Pragmatic Research 7
   1.6 Consciousness-Raising Hypothesis 7
   1.7 Noticing Hypothesis 8
   1.8 Speech Acts 8
      1.8.1 Request 9
      1.8.2 Apology 9
      1.8.3 Refusal 10
   1.9 Meta-Analysis 10
   References 11

2 **Review of Previous Research** 17
   2.1 Introduction 17
   2.2 Recent Studies on the Instruction of the Speech Acts of Request, Apology, and Refusal 17
   2.3 Previous Reviews and Meta-Analyses in L2 Pragmatic 22
   2.4 Conclusion 28
   References 28

3 **Methodology** 31
   3.1 Introduction 31
   3.2 Research Questions 31
   3.3 Research Design 32
   3.4 Study Identification and Retrieval 32
   3.5 Inclusion and Exclusion Criteria 33
   3.6 Effect Size Calculation 34
   3.7 Coding of Moderator Variables 34
   3.8 Missing Data 36

	3.9	Reliability	36
	3.10	Publication Bias	36
	References		37
4	**Results**		**39**
	4.1	Introduction	39
	4.2	Description of the Included Corpus	39
		4.2.1 Effect Size Frequency for the Speech Act Variable	39
		4.2.2 Effect Size Frequency for the Outcome Measure Variable	50
		4.2.3 Effect Size Frequency for Treatment Type Variable	51
		4.2.4 Effect Size Frequency for the Psycholinguistic Feature Variable	52
		4.2.5 Effect Size Frequency for the Age Variable	52
		4.2.6 Effect Size Frequency for the Gender Variable	53
		4.2.7 Effect Size Frequency for the Proficiency Level Variable	54
		4.2.8 Effect Size Frequency for the Design Variable	55
	4.3	Overall Effectiveness of L2 Pragmatic Instruction	55
		4.3.1 Main Results	55
		4.3.2 Publication Bias	59
	4.4	Overall Effectiveness of L2 Pragmatic Instruction on the Speech Act of Apology	60
		4.4.1 Main Results for the Effectiveness of Instruction Focused on Apology	60
		4.4.2 Publication Bias	61
	4.5	Overall Effectiveness of L2 Pragmatic Instruction on the Speech Act of Refusal	64
		4.5.1 Main Results for the Effectiveness of Instruction Focused on Refusals	64
		4.5.2 Publication Bias	66
	4.6	Overall Effectiveness of L2 Pragmatic Instruction on the Speech Act of Request	67
		4.6.1 Main Results of the Effectiveness of Instruction Focused on Request	67
		4.6.2 Publication Bias	70
	4.7	Moderating Effects of L2 Pragmatic Instruction	71
		4.7.1 Demographic Features	71
		4.7.2 Design-Related Features	75
	References		79

5	**Discussion**	85
	5.1 Introduction	85
	5.2 Research Question 1: What is the Overall Effectiveness of the Instruction of L2 Pragmatics, Particularly the Speech Acts of Request, Apology, and Refusal?	86
	5.3 Research Question 2: What are the Variables Which Moderate the Effectiveness of L2 Pragmatic Instruction, Especially the Speech Acts of Request, Apology, and Refusal?	88
	References	90
6	**Conclusions, Limitations, Pedagogical Implications, and Directions for Future Research**	93
	6.1 Introduction	93
	6.2 Limitations	93
	6.3 Implications	94
	6.4 Directions for Future Research	95
	6.5 Conclusions	96
	References	97
Appendix: Results for All Studies Included		99

Chapter 1
Overview of the Theoretical Frameworks

1.1 Introduction

Globalization has provided the urge for people to communicate with each other during the last few decades (Derakhshan & Shakki, 2020b), and considering the advancement of globalization, English language teaching has been increasingly emphasized in many countries. It is believed that English proficiency is a vital component of global communication in tourism, business, information technology, and other domains (Kubota & McKay, 2009). According to Dewaele (2010), meaningful communication among foreign language users is closely linked to their knowledge of lexis, grammar, syntax, phonology, and also pragmatics.

It can be concluded that communication requires appropriate knowledge of the target language skills; therefore, language teaching receives much attention, and instruction is considered a panacea for increasing learners' perception of the target language (Cohen & Ishihara, 2013; Félix-Brasdefer, 2008; Ishihara & Cohen, 2010, 2014; Takahashi, 2013, 2015). The rudimentary goal of language teaching is to develop communication skills in the language-learning process (Bardovi-Harlig, 2022). Hence, being a competent speaker involves acquiring knowledge beyond the correct usage of the grammar, lexis, and pronunciation rules of the language being learned (Alcón-Soler & Martínez-Flor, 2008; Taguchi, 2019; van Compernolle, 2014). It also includes understanding how language must be used in various situations (Shakki et al., 2021; Youn, 2018). This knowledge enables learners to go beyond the literal meaning of a statement to interpret the intended purpose and use appropriate language to avoid misunderstandings or being viewed as rude or disrespectful (Félix-Brasdefer & Koike, 2012; González-Lloret, 2020).

Most language learners experience anxiety along with the need to communicate with other native and non-native speakers once they enter the target language environment (Bardovi-Harlig et al., 2015; Barron, 2016). As was defined by MacIntyre and Gardner (1994), foreign language anxiety is a feeling of apprehension associated with foreign language contexts, and it includes listening, speaking, and learning.

Language users often feel that their grammar and vocabulary means are inadequate for full participation in an interaction, and they lack the intuition of a native speaker about what is appropriate, polite, and acceptable in the target culture (González-Lloret & Ortega, 2018). This is where pragmatics comes into play with the "What, with whom, when, where, [and] how we speak" (Hymes, 1972, p. 60) playing a role in our ability to communicate successfully in a second or foreign language.

Pragmatics has been introduced as the study of the relationship among the signs of the interpreters, and it has been defined as one of the most fertile grounds for research (Morris, 1938). Taguchi (2019) believes that learning linguistic norms and acquiring sociocultural conventions are essential constituents of becoming a proficient L2 speaker. It is thought that interaction should also be constructed by discourse among the participants. Young (2011) postulates that people use an amalgamation of interactional resources during the interaction, such as speech acts, topic management, register-specific linguistic forms, repair, and turn-taking. These resources are shared among the participants to manipulate the communicative act.

Pragmatic competence has achieved prominence as a newly developed branch of linguistics during the last decades (Fraser, 2010). Pragmatic competence concerns the ability to address a complicated interplay among language, the context of the interaction, and language users (Kondo, 1997). Correspondingly, Interlanguage Pragmatics (ILP) is a comparatively nascent area in linguistics that derived its origin from pragmatic theory and developments in L2 research and pedagogy in the 1970s (Derakhshan & Shakki, 2021). ILP is the study of how learners, whether children or adults, acquire the ability to produce and understand communicative action in L2 and has its base in the theories of pragmatic and L2 acquisition under the influence of Hymes' (1971, 1972) communicative competence (Kasper & Blum-Kulka, 1993). Hymes (1971) envisions that a speaker's communicative competence encompasses four types of knowledge that take into account their ability to estimate to what extent an utterance is (a) grammatically possible, (b) cognitively feasible, (c) socially and culturally appropriate, and (d) actually performed.

ILP is a hybrid discipline that is the result of the marriage of pragmatics and Second Language Acquisition (SLA) research focusing on pragmatics and SLA theories, structures, and principles to scrutinize how language learners in foreign or second language contexts create and recreate meaning in their L2, with major emphasis being placed on speech acts, conversational routines, and implicature (Derakhshan & Eslami, 2020). Considering what Kasper and Rose (1999, 2002) found, we know that pragmatics is amenable to teaching, and instructed groups often outperformed non-instructed groups. This is in line with what Ellis (2008) reported about instruction. He cogently argued that more input could lead to more opportunities to produce output and better language learning. Moreover, it has been found that as the teachers' support and instruction in the class increase, learners' engagement and learning will be augmented (Shakki, 2022a). This highlights the teachers' role and generates a central impetus for learning (Derakhshan & Shakki, 2019).

Reviewing the previous findings on pragmatics has illustrated slow pragmatic development in different real-life contexts (Taguchi, 2019) and accentuated how essential it is to concentrate on pragmatics instruction (Derakhshan, 2019, 2020).

1.1 Introduction

The majority of scholars believe that pragmatic features, like other language skills such as grammar and vocabulary, should be incorporated into classroom pedagogy.

Researchers have examined the effectiveness of different instructional methods, such as input- and output-based instruction, explicit and implicit teaching, meta-pragmatic discussion, skill acquisition and practice, and teaching within the Zone of Proximal Development (hereafter ZPD) (Cohen, 2008; Culpeper et al., 2018; Derakhshan & Cohen, 2021; Derakhshan & Eslami, 2015, 2019, 2020; Derakhshan & Malmir, 2021; Derakhshan & Shakki, 2020a, 2021; Derakhshan et al., 2020; Hernández, 2021; Irshad & Bukhari, 2020; Jeon & Kaya, 2006; Kasper & Roever, 2005; Kasper & Rose, 1999, 2002; Malmir & Derakhshan, 2020; Martínez-Flor & Alcón-Soler, 2005; Plonsky & Zhuang, 2019; Rose, 2005; Schauer, 2022; Shakki et al., 2020; Sykes, 2009; Sykes & Dubreil, 2019; Tajeddin & Alemi, 2020; Takahashi, 2010a, 2010b; Taguchi, 2011, 2015, 2019; Vygotsky, 1987; Wang & Ren, 2022; Zangoie & Derakhshan, 2021). In most of these studies, findings show the positive effects of instruction and its superiority.

Additionally, researchers have found the existence of sampling error in individual studies problematic, leading to mixed results. An established methodology can solve this issue when more research is done in a particular field of study (Hunter & Schmidt, 2004). Considering this problem, the cumulation of findings of primary studies was found to be the only solution to overcome the presence of sampling error. Glass (1976) posited meta-analysis as a remedy to handle this issue, and Li (2010) introduced meta-analysis as "a quantitative review of the research on the effect of the certain treatment on a response variable" (p. 312). The purpose of a meta-analysis is to review, summarize, then add new knowledge (Hall et al., 1994). Moreover, this type of analysis organizes the findings of primary studies via a numerical index of effect size, then compares and mixes the results to reach a final conclusion. Finally, regarding Hedges (1992), meta-analysis has gained momentum in many fields of study, such as psychology, education, and sciences, to check the effectiveness of a variable by combining the results of the primary studies.

Meta-analyses have been recognized as a productive way to consider the results of preliminary studies, and applying them in education and language studies has been proposed (Oswald & Plonsky, 2010). Because of its pivotal place in language learning, instruction has received much attention, and its effectiveness has been under question for a couple of centuries. The supremacy of meta-analysis in relation to other methods was identified after Norris and Ortega's (2000) seminal work on the effectiveness of instruction. After that, many studies were conducted using meta-analyses on a variety of research topics, such as writing (Graham et al., 2012), feedback (Russell & Spada, 2006), form-focused instruction (Kang et al., 2019), and construct validity of language aptitude (Li, 2016).

An overview of existing meta-analyses has indicated that the overall effectiveness of the instruction of pragmatics for the speech acts of request, apology, and refusal has received scant attention; instead, these speech acts have only been studied using some moderators in an Iranian context (Shakki et al., 2020, 2021). The present book aims to review the previous studies to find the effectiveness of instruction for these speech acts worldwide. Its goal is also to identify the moderator variables that can predict this effectiveness. However, this meta-analysis cannot be regarded as a profitable endeavor unless it considers all the key concepts in pragmatics instruction, such as age, gender, proficiency, outcome measures, etc. Moreover, since the present study intermingles the most frequent speech acts of request, apology, and refusal, it may provide a broader view for researchers and prognosticate areas that have yet to be studied.

1.2 Instructed Second Language Acquisition

Acquiring a rule-based competence, including the knowledge of grammatical rules and a rich collection of formulaic expressions which cater to accuracy and fluency, are the prerequisites for proficiency in an L2 (East, 2017; Halenko, 2021; Skehan, 1998). It has been shown that native speakers use a much larger number of formulaic expressions than speakers who claim to be advanced in L2 learning (Foster-Cohen, 2001), which is why those expressions are considered a basis for developing a rule-based competence. To be native-like speakers, learners seek ways they can improve their language skills through instruction (Ellis, 2005).

Moreover, it is vital to use appropriate instructional approaches for semantic and pragmatic meaning. While both teachers and learners view language as an object, from a pragmatic meaning point of view, they need to treat language as a tool for communication (Ellis, 2005). Regarding the importance of pragmatic meaning, many theorists (Prabhu, 1987; Long, 1996) believe that pragmatic acquisition will take place when the learners are involved in decoding and encoding the messages in the context of actual acts. This means that learners must have opportunities to engage in some activities in which the pragmatic meaning is intrinsically motivating to create this kind of meaning (DeKeyser, 1998).

Furthermore, this instruction paves the way in the process of SLA and also Foreign Language Acquisition (FLA) to provide those opportunities through which learning will happen. During the last decades, there have been several studies in which the definition of Instructed Second Language Acquisition (ISLA) was described (Ellis, 2008; Housen et al., 2005). However, the most recent explanation can be found in Loewen (2015) who stated that ISLA is a field of academic research that is based on theoretical and empirical background and whose purpose is to provide systematic manipulation of the mechanisms of learning and the situation under which learning happens to facilitate the development and the acquisition of additional languages.

This simple definition of ISLA focuses on a key component, the systematic manipulation of the learning processes. This is the most crucial factor distinguishing instructed from uninstructed or naturalistic L2 acquisition. In ISLA, systematic attempts are made by learners or teachers to develop L2, while in naturalistic L2 acquisition, this development occurs as a result of exposure to the target language. L2 proficiency can be achieved in both types of acquisitions. However, the difference is that in the second group, learners are not actively involved in the process of language learning, and they are not concerned with language acquisition (Loewen & Sato, 2017).

Taking ISLA into account, a preliminary question needs to be answered: What is the best way to learn a second or foreign language? While Krashen (1982) believes instruction may have little impact unless it is provided with authentic materials, most ISLA researchers corroborate that instruction of any sort can be positive and significant (Derakhshan & Shakki, 2021; García-Gómez, 2022; Loewen & Sato, 2017; Sánchez-Hernández & Martínez-Flor, 2022; Zhang, 2022). Bearing in mind the role of meaning in form-focused instruction, many researchers in ISLA studies aim to make learners capable of using the language for communicative purposes (Littlewood, 2014). This fact highlights the relationship between instruction and pragmatics, which is very important and leads to language competency.

1.3 Models of Communicative Competence and Pragmatics

Different scholars have emphasized the construct of communicative competence. Inspired by Hymes's (1971, 1972) postulations criticizing Chomsky's (1957) linguistic competence, it was Canale and Swain (1980) who posited the first and the most influential model of what they called "communicative competence" as comprising grammatical competence, sociolinguistic competence, strategic competence, and discoursal knowledge. Each of the subcategories has its own definition as follows: grammatical competence has been defined as the ability to produce grammatically correct utterances; sociolinguistic competence is the ability to create sociolinguistically appropriate utterances; strategic competence is the ability to solve communication problems, and finally, discourse knowledge is the ability to generate cohesive and coherent utterances (Canale & Swain, 1980; Sharwood Smith, 1993).

Bachman (1990) explicitly mentioned the pragmatic component under the rubric of "pragmatic competence". The author makes a distinction between pragmatic competence and organizational competence. Moreover, as seen in Fig. 1.1, Bachman (1990) conceptualizes two more constitutes of communicative language ability, strategic and psychomotor skills. The former allows language users to draw on the items included within language competence. The latter deals with the productive or receptive mode in which competence is performed through a special type of channel.

1.4 Defining Pragmatics and Interlanguage Pragmatics

Pragmatics has been defined as "the study of speaker and hearer meaning created in their joint actions that include both linguistic and non-linguistic signals in the context of socioculturally organized activities" (LoCastro, 2013, p. 5). While dating back to philosophical thinking in the early nineteenth century, pragmatics has gradually attempted to establish its specific status in the world academic arena. Pragmatics

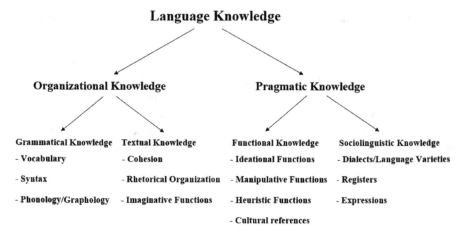

Fig. 1.1 Bachman's (1990) model of communicative competence (p. 94)

can be analyzed from two perspectives: the sociocultural-interactional view through which speakers' messages and interlocutors' responses are taken into account, and the cognitive-philosophical view in which pragmatics is considered as a component of mental grammar and includes concepts like speech acts and conversational implicature (van Compernolle, 2014). It is a fast-growing system characterized by numerous research outputs, and since concepts such as presuppositions are problematic in semantic analysis, there remains a need for a pragmatic solution. Moreover, a number of phenomena, such as pragmatic markers ("well", "anyhow") and interjections or vocatives, are seen to be interpreted and analyzed through the pragmatics view.

ILP, motivated by SLA theories and pragmatics, is concerned with how L2 learners learn to do things with words over time in their own country. It deals with how learners (adults or children) learn to find out and produce communicative actions in a second language, and as an interdisciplinary field, it has been studied from various methodological, theoretical, and analytical perspectives. Asking a professor to write a recommendation letter, complaining about a grade on an exam, refusing an offer, and knowing when it is suitable to be reticent in a conversation are some examples of ILP. This term is closely interconnected with pragmatic competence, which in turn is one of the significant components of communicative competence in different developed models like Canale and Swain (1980) and Bachman and Palmer (1996, 2010). One aspect of learners' communicative competence is pragmatic knowledge, including pragmalinguistic and sociopragmatic knowledge. Knowing different forms and their meanings can be a subcategory of pragmalinguistic in which a person can refuse an offer by saying "I cannot". Considering the expressions which are appropriate to use can also be a subarea for sociopragmatic.

1.5 Cognitive Approaches in L2 Pragmatic Research

As Ellis (2008) cogently states, cognitive approaches to L2 acquisition concentrate on learners' internal mechanisms, which deal with acquiring and representing L2 knowledge. According to this understanding, two areas of research are suggested. The first area scrutinizes the nature of L2 knowledge (e.g., declarative vs. procedural, explicit vs. implicit). The second investigates the cognitive processes (e.g., monitoring, attention, and restructuring) involved in cognitive knowledge acquisition (i.e., development of the mental representation of knowledge). As accentuated by Ellis (2008), cognitive SLA expressly confirms issues regarding knowledge representation (skill acquisition theories and Bialystok's two-dimensional model) or issues related to cognitive processes (Schmidt, 1993, 2001). Cognitive orientation, reinforced by Kasper and Blum-Kulka's (1993) edited volume, features cognitive theories. Though the field has witnessed an amalgamation of theoretical orientations, the "cognitivist" stance remains a solid presence among alternative theoretical approaches (Kasper & Rose, 2002; Taguchi & Roever, 2017).

1.6 Consciousness-Raising Hypothesis

The term *consciousness-raising* displays purposeful attention that is given to the formal possessions of language and it intends to enhance second language development. Sharwood Smith (1993) claims that "consciousness-raising implies that the learner's mental state is altered by the input; hence, all input is intake" (p. 176). Ellis (2002) explains that consciousness-raising aims to help the learners know about the language and particularly, specific structures, but not to enable them to perform structures correctly. Accordingly, there are some important features of consciousness-raising that should be highlighted in applying it for the fulfillment of this goal. In performing consciousness-raising tasks, the learners are expected to express the rule and utilize intellectual effort to perceive the language structures.

Moreover, in order to have focused attention, learners are provided with specific language features in an explicit way with subtle explanations. There are also some techniques through which consciousness-raising tasks can be executed, one of which is the identification that was explicitly explained by Ellis (2002) as a prerequisite for learners to look for a set of data to realize a pattern of usage. After identification, language users have to classify the data regarding the differences and similarities. In another technique, hypothesis building/checking, learners make a generalization of the data and check this generalization according to the target form. Then, in the next stage which is cross-language exploration, learners should search for the differences and similarities between the English language and their language. Finally, language users are recommended to reconstruct the elements of language in the recall stage, and they are encouraged to use the resources during the discovery activities such as grammar references, study guides, or dictionaries in the last technique which is called reference training (Willis & Willis, 2007). All of the mentioned techniques are used to make learners aware of language features, so they become ready to receive instruction.

1.7 Noticing Hypothesis

Schmidt (2001) believes that even if students are provided with enough input or exposure of any kind but are not made aware of the sociopragmatic and pragmalinguistic features of the input, they cannot develop their ILP. Schmidt (1993, 2001) cogently propounds that according to psycholinguistic theory and research on L2 learning, input ought to be noticed or detected under attention for it to be acquisitionally germane. Schmidt (2001) elaborates that global awareness of target language input is inadequate; instead, attention must be allotted to specific learning objects. He further states that "in order to acquire pragmatics, one must attend to both the linguistic forms of utterances and the relevant social and contextual features with which they are associated" (p. 30). Schmidt (1995) further makes a demarcation between noticing and understanding.

Noticing is defined as the "conscious registration of the occurrence of some event," while understanding purports "the recognition of some general principle, rule, or pattern. Noticing refers to the surface level phenomena and item learning, while understanding refers to the deeper level(s) of abstraction related to (semantic, syntactic, or communicative) meaning, system learning" (p. 29). Like other theoretical constructs, noticing, one of the most frequently referenced theories in second language pragmatics research, has some implications for pragmatics development. Firstly, the hypothesis (strong version) prognosticates that no pragmatic development happens without the presence of attention. Secondly, it (weak version) corroborates the fact that more attention leads to more pragmatics learning. Thirdly, understanding seems to result in better learning than just noticing the concepts.

1.8 Speech Acts

Since the incorporation of language functions in the notional-functional syllabus in the 1970s (Wilkins, 1972), speech acts have attracted considerable attention in SLA in general and ILP in particular. A myriad of studies have scrutinized speech acts and the effect of various interventional treatments on the production and comprehension of different speech acts within the domain of SLA. Speech acts are utterances that perform a locutionary and an illocutionary meaning in daily communications (Derakhshan et al., 2021; Ellis, 2008). They are well suited to a formulaic lexical approach to language. This idea is corroborated by Cohen (2008), who states that speech acts reflect the equally routinized language and facilitate language learning by enhancing the predictability of speech. According to Reimann (2011), speech acts should be regarded as social parameters of communication and are the main chunks of language suitable for particular contexts, tasks, or events. Speech acts are of different kinds, such as request, apology, refusal, complaint, compliment, etc., among which request, apology, and refusal have been chosen to be investigated and elaborated on in the present study.

1.8.1 Request

The study of speech acts has received a great deal of attention in empirical research. The requesting speech act is one such speech act that needs further investigation as it has been recognized as the most dominant speech act (Félix-Brasdefer, 2007; Shakki et al., 2020). A request is "an attempt to get the listener to do something" (Searle, 1976, p. 3). It is the speaker's effort to ask the addressee to do something or not to do something. Brown and Levinson (1987) consider verbal prompting a face-threatening act (FTA). They classify this speech act as an FTA because the speaker imposes "freedom of action" on the listener. To reduce the degree of impudence towards recipients and minimize facial threats, speakers use specific query strategies (Blum-Kulka, 1982; Sykes, 2009). In their project "Cross-Cultural Study of Realization Patterns of Speech Acts (CCSARP)", Blum-Kulka (1991) divide the query sequence into three parts: 'Alerters', 'Head Act', and 'Supportive Moves'. The purpose of dividing the command utterance act into these three segments is to identify the utterance that is the "core of the head act" (Blum-Kulka & Olshtain, 1984, p. 200).

It is claimed that the request can be fulfilled from four different angles: Avoidance of any of these elements by referring to the perspective of the listener, the perspective of the speaker, the perspective of both participants, or only the action being performed (Blum-Kulka & Olshtain, 1984, p. 201). In addition, Blum-Kulka and Olshtain (1984) distinguish four categories:

1. Listener Oriented:
   Could you open the door?
2. Speaker directivity:
   May I borrow your laptop?
3. Speaker and Listener Orientation:
   Could you please edit this paper?
4. Impersonal:
   It might be a good idea to open the windows.

1.8.2 Apology

An apology is a means of compensating for actions that violate sociocultural norms. As emotional acts (Searle, 1975), apologies are a fundamental component of our social existence because they enable everyone to fulfill their moral responsibilities while helping to maintain harmony among people (Norrick, 1978). According to Fraser (1981), "To apologize means to do two things: take responsibility for offensive behavior and express regret for crimes committed". Apologizing is an example of "action in favor of a socially sanctioned healer" (Edmondson, 1981, p. 280). Attempts to restore social harmony and interpersonal balance are associated with behaviors that offend others and making an apology "after the fact" (Bergman & Kasper, 1993).

There are different types of strategies that learners can use to apologize for what they have done, ranging from more direct ("I apologize for…", "I want to apologize for…") to less direct ("I apologize for…"). "I'm sorry…"; "I'm sorry…") (Blum-Kulka, 1991; Fraser, 1981). These can focus on acknowledging responsibility for actions ("It was my fault"), offering compensation ("I will bear the damage"), and asking for forgiveness ("I'm sorry") or a strategy aimed at generous promises, ("It will never happen again") if the crime could happen again (Fraser, 1981). These strategies can be prosodically, lexically, and syntactically upgraded or downgraded to modify speech power. For example, "I'm sorry" can be lexically modified with "that way" or "really" as a general expression of regret.

1.8.3 Refusal

Performance of refusals can range substantially depending on sociolinguistic elements such as the reputation or the context of those who are involved in the interaction, and it calls for appropriate techniques to limit the negative impact on the interlocutor. Refusals can contain a lengthy collection of interactional exchanges. At the same time, the linguistic technique used to perform a refusal can change depending on whether or not one is refusing an invitation, an offer, or a request (Beebe et al., 1990; Salazar Campillo et al., 2009). Refusal techniques can be categorized into direct techniques, oblique techniques, and adjuncts to refusals. Direct techniques consist of a blunt "no" and negation (e.g., "I can't" or "I don't assume so"). Indirect techniques consist of suggesting different options, explanations, and avoidance. Adjuncts to refusals are external changes of the speech act. They consist of expressions of gratitude, consent, empathy, or a statement of positive opinion or feeling (Krulatz & Dixon, 2020). Unlike different speech acts, including requests, complaints, and apologies, refusals have received little interest and attention in studies on interlanguage pragmatics.

1.9 Meta-Analysis

Meta-analysis has been recognized as an emerging research method, and its advantages over other approaches, such as the narrative method or vote-counting method, have been recognized (Borenstein et al., 2021). The history of meta-analyses dates back to long ago, with the first drafts released in the 1930s. According to Crombie and Davies (2009), meta-analyses can be of two kinds; they may deal with the combination of hypotheses or the combination of estimates. Although it is widespread in medical sciences, this new method has not been adequately utilized in language fields; hence, conducting meta-analyses in this field of study is recommended. Some advantages of conducting meta-analyses include that they are done rigorously, thereby reducing publication bias, and the dramatic effects can easily be detected (Derakhshan & Shakki, 2021). Second, meta-analyses can provide a lucid picture of the variable through metaregression since it uses the aggregation of data instead of a few participants. Finally, the transparency of meta-analyses is another positive point justifying the rationality of the decisions taken through the process of finding the effect sizes (Crombie & Davies, 2009).

The term "meta-analysis" was first introduced by Gene Glass in 1976. It was defined as the analysis of the analyses, which refers to the statistical analysis of an extensive collection of findings from individual studies. In each meta-analysis, some specific phases must be followed so as to expand the knowledge of the field. First, the relevant studies need to be identified and collected. Second, the researchers must generate some inclusion and exclusion criteria based on which of the primary studies are categorized. The remaining studies are required to be coded according to the important criteria for further analysis. The coding schema may be similar to previous studies on the same topic, or the researchers may have their own coding procedure. Third, the effect size of the studies must be extracted by Comprehensive Meta-Analysis Software (CMA). Finally, the data analysis is run to scrutinize the effectiveness of the variable or the moderating variables. A meta-analysis should be considered when researchers plan to present a systematic, comprehensive, and quantitative study in which the findings of the previous studies are all resembled and presented.

References

Alcón-Soler, E., & Martínez-Flor, A. (Eds.). (2008). *Investigating pragmatics in foreign language learning, teaching and testing.* Multilingual Matters.

Bachman, L. F. (1990). *Fundamental considerations in language testing.* Oxford University Press.

Bachman, L. F., & Palmer, A. S. (1996). *Language testing in practice: Designing and developing useful language tests.* Oxford University Press.

Bachman, L. F., & Palmer, A. S. (2010). *Language assessment in practice.* Oxford University Press.

Bardovi-Harlig, K. (2022). Pragmatics: Speaking as a pragmalinguistic resource. In *The Routledge handbook of second language acquisition and speaking* (pp. 243–257). Routledge.

Bardovi-Harlig, K., Mossman, S., & Vellenga, H. E. (2015). The effect of instruction on pragmatic routines in academic discussion. *Language Teaching Research, 19*, 324–350.

Barron, A. (2016). Developing pragmatic competence using EFL textbooks: Focus on requests. *Literacy Information and Computer Education Journal (LICEJ), 7*, 2172–2179.

Beebe, L. M., Takahashi, T., & Uliss-Weltz, R. (1990). Pragmatic transfer in ESL refusals. In R. Scarcella, E. Andersen, & S. Krashen (Eds.), *Developing communicative competence in a second language* (pp. 55–73). Newbury House.

Bergman, M. L., & Kasper, G. (1993). Perception and performance in native and nonnative apology. In G. Kasper & S. Blum-Kulka (Eds.), *Interlanguage pragmatics* (pp. 82–107). Oxford University Press.

Blum-Kulka, S. (1982). Learning to say what you mean in a second language: A study of speech act performance of learners of Hebrew as a second language. *Applied Linguistics, 3*(1), 29–59.

Blum-Kulka, S. (1991). Interlanguage pragmatics: The case of requests. In R. Phillipson, E. Kellerman, L. Selinker, M. Smith, & M. Swain (Eds.), *Foreign/second language pedagogy research—A commemorative volume for Claus Faerch* (pp. 255–272). Multilingual Matters.

Blum-Kulka, S., & Olshtain, E. (1984). Requests and apologies: A cross-cultural study of speech act realization patterns (CCSARP). *Applied Linguistics, 5*(3), 196–213.

Borenstein, M., Hedges, L. V., Higgins, J. P., & Rothstein, H. R. (2021). *Introduction to meta-analysis*. Wiley.

Brown, P., & Levinson, S. C. (1987). *Politeness: Some universals in language usage* (Vol. 4). Cambridge University Press.

Canale, M., & Swain, M. (1980). Theoretical aspects of communicative approaches to second language teaching and testing. *Applied Linguistics, 1*(1), 1–47.

Chomsky, N. (1957). *Syntactic structures*. Mouton de Gruyter.

Cohen, A. D. (2008). Teaching and assessing L2 pragmatics: What can we expect from learners? *Language Teaching, 41*(2), 213–235.

Cohen, A. D., & Ishihara, N. (2013). Pragmatics. In B. Tomlinson (Ed.), *Applied linguistics and materials development* (pp. 113–126). Bloomsbury.

Crombie, I. K., & Davies, H. T. (2009). What is meta-analysis. *What Is, 1*(8), 1–18.

Culpeper, J., Mackey, A., & Taguchi, N. (2018). *Second language pragmatics: From theory to research*. Routledge.

DeKeyser, R. M. (1998). Beyond focus on form: Cognitive perspectives on learning and practicing second language grammar. In C. Doughty & J. Williams (Eds.), *Focus on form in classroom second language acquisition* (pp. 42–63). Cambridge University Press.

Derakhshan, A. (2019). Review of the book *The Routledge handbook of second language acquisition and pragmatics*, by N. Taguchi. *Applied Linguistics*. https://doi.org/10.1093/applin/amz031

Derakhshan, A. (2020). Review of the book *Tasks, pragmatics and multilingualism in the classroom: A portrait of adolescent writing in multiple languages*, by S. Martín-Laguna. *Journal of Pragmatics, 168*, 53–56.

Derakhshan, A., & Cohen, A.D. (2021). Introduction to the TESL-EJ: Special issue on teaching, learning, assessing, and researching L2 pragmatics in honor of Prof. Zohreh R. Eslami. *TESL-EJ, 25*(1). http://www.tesl-ej.org/wordpress/issues/volume25/ej97/ej97a0/

Derakhshan, A., & Eslami, Z. R. (2015). The effect of consciousness-raising instruction on the comprehension of apology & request. *TESL-EJ, 18*(4). http://www.tesl-ej.org/wordpress/issues/volume18/ej72/ej72a6/

Derakhshan, A., & Eslami, Z. R. (2019). Review of the book *Second language pragmatics: From theory to research*, by J. Culpeper, A. Mackey, & N. Taguchi. *Intercultural Pragmatics, 16*(5), 611–617.

Derakhshan, A., & Eslami, Z. R. (2020). The effect of metapragmatic awareness, interactive translation, and discussion through video-enhanced input on EFL learners' comprehension of implicature. *Applied Research on English Language, 9*(1), 25–52. https://doi.org/10.22108/are.2019.118062.1476

Derakhshan, A., & Malmir, A. (2021). The role of language aptitude in the development of L2 pragmatic competence. *TESL-EJ, 25*(1), 1–30. http://www.tesl-ej.org/wordpress/issues/volume25/ej97/ej97a0/

Derakhshan, A., Malmir, A., & Greenier, V. (2021). Interlanguage pragmatic learning strategies (IPLS) as predictors of L2 speech act knowledge: A case of Iranian EFL learners. *The Journal of Asia TEFL, 18*(1), 235–243. https://doi.org/10.18823/asiatefl.2021.18.1.14.235

Derakhshan, A., & Shakki, F. (2019). A critical review of language teacher education for a global society: A modular model for knowing, analyzing, recognizing, doing, and seeing. *Critical*

References

Studies in Texts & Programs of Human Sciences and Council for the Study of Humanities Texts and Books, 19(6), 109–127.

Derakhshan, A., & Shakki, F. (2020a). The effect of implicit vs. explicit metapragmatic instruction on the Iranian intermediate EFL learners' pragmatic comprehension of apology and refusal. *Journal of Language Research, 12*(37), 151–175.

Derakhshan, A., & Shakki, F. (2020b). Review of the book *Worldwide English language education today: ideologies, policies, and practices*, by A. Al-Issa & S. A. Mirhosseini. *System, 90*, 102224. https://doi.org/10.1016/j.system.2020.102224

Derakhshan, A., & Shakki, F. (2021). A meta-analytic study of instructed second language pragmatics: A case of the speech act of request. *Journal of Research in Applied Linguistics, 12*(1), 15–32. https://doi.org/10.22055/RALS.2021.16722

Derakhshan, A., Shakki, F., & Sarani, M. A. (2020). The effect of dynamic and non-dynamic assessment on the comprehension of Iranian intermediate EFL learners' speech acts of apology and request. *Language Related Research, 11*(4), 605–637.

Dewaele, J.-M. (2010). Multilingualism and affordances: Variation in self-perceived communicative competence and communicative anxiety in French L1, L2, L3 and L4. *International Review of Applied Linguistics, 48*, 105–129.

East, M. (2017). Research into practice: The task-based approach to instructed second language acquisition. *Language Teaching, 50*(3), 412–424.

Edmondson, W. J. (1981). On saying you're sorry. In F. Coulmas (Ed.), *Conversational routine: Explorations in standardized communication situations and prepatterned speech* (pp. 273–288). Mouton.

Ellis, R. (2002). Grammar teaching: Practice or consciousness-raising? In J. C. Richard & W. A. Renandya (Eds.), *Methodology in language teaching: An anthology of current practice* (pp. 167–174). Cambridge University Press.

Ellis, R. (2005). Principles of instructed language learning. *System, 33*(2), 209–224.

Ellis, R. (2008). *The study of second language acquisition*. Oxford University Press.

Félix-Brasdefer, J. C. (2007). Pragmatic development in the Spanish as a FL classroom: A cross-sectional study of learner requests. *Intercultural Pragmatics, 4*(2), 253–286.

Félix-Brasdefer, J. C. (2008). Teaching pragmatics in the classroom: Instruction of mitigation in Spanish as a foreign language. *Hispania, 91*, 479–494.

Félix-Brasdefer, J. C., & Koike, D. (2012). Introduction: Pragmatic variation in first and second language contexts. In J. C. Félix-Brasdefer & D. Koike (Eds.), *Pragmatic variation in first and second language contexts: Methodological issues* (pp. 1–15). John Benjamins.

Foster-Cohen, S. (2001). First language acquisition... second language acquisition: 'What's Hecuba to him or he to Hecuba?'. *Second Language Research, 17*(4), 329–344.

Fraser, B. (1981). On apologizing. In F. Coulmas (Ed.), *Conversational routine: Explorations in standardized communication situations and prepatterned speech* (pp. 259–271). Mouton.

Fraser, B. (2010). Pragmatic competence: The case of hedging. In G. Kaltenböck, W. Mihatsch, & S. Schneider (Eds.), *New approaches to hedging* (pp. 15–34). Emerald.

García-Gómez, A. (2022). Learning through WhatsApp: Students' beliefs, L2 pragmatic development and interpersonal relationships. *Computer Assisted Language Learning, 35*(5–6), 1310–1328.

Glass, G. (1976). Primary, secondary, and meta-analysis of research. *Education Researcher, 5*(10), 3–8.

González-Lloret, M. (2020). Pragmatic development in L2: An overview. In K. P. Schneider & E. Ifantidou (Eds.), *Handbook of developmental and clinical Pragmatics*. Mouton de Gruyter.

González-Lloret, M., & Ortega, L. (2018). Pragmatics, tasks, and technology: A synergy. In N. Taguchi & Y. Kim (Eds.), *Task-based approaches to teaching and assessing pragmatics* (pp. 191–216). John Benjamins.

Graham, S., McKeown, D., Kiuhara, S., & Harris, K. R. (2012). A meta-analysis of writing instruction for students in the elementary grades. *Journal of Educational Psychology, 104*(4), 1–18.

Halenko, N. (2021). *Teaching pragmatics and instructed second language learning.* Bloomsbury.

Hall, J. A., Tickle-Degnen, L., Rosenthal, R., & Mosteller, F. (1994). Hypotheses and problems in research synthesis. In H. Cooper & L. V. Hedges (Eds.), *The handbook of research synthesis* (pp. 17–28). Russell Sage Foundation.

Hedges, L. V. (1992). Meta-analysis. *Journal of Educational Statistics, 17*(4), 279–296.

Hernández, T. A. (2021). Explicit instruction for the development of L2 Spanish pragmatic ability during study abroad. *System, 96*, 102395. https://doi.org/10.1016/j.system.2020.102395

Housen, A., Pierrard, M., & Van Daele, S. (2005). Rule complexity and the efficacy of explicit grammar instruction. In A. Housen & M. Pierrard (Eds.), *Investigation in instructed language acquisition* (pp. 235–269). Mouton de Gruyter.

Hunter, J. E., & Schmidt, F. L. (2004). *Methods of meta-analysis: Correcting error and bias in research findings.* Sage.

Hymes, D. (1971). Competence and performance in linguistic theory. In R. Huxley & E. Ingram (Eds.), *Language acquisition: Models and methods* (pp. 3–28). Academic Press.

Hymes, D. (1972). On communicative competence. In J. Pride & J. Holmes (Eds.), *Sociolinguistics* (pp. 269–293). Penguin Books.

Irshad, A., & Bukhari, N. H. (2020). Investigating the effect of explicit instruction on the development of pragmatic competence of Pakistani learners of English. *Kashmir Journal of Language Research, 23*(1), 217–236.

Ishihara, N., & Cohen, A. D. (2010). *Teaching and learning pragmatics: Where language and culture meet.* Pearson Longman.

Ishihara, N., & Cohen, A. D. (2014). *Teaching and learning pragmatics: Where language and culture meet.* Routledge.

Jeon, E. H., & Kaya, T. (2006). Effects of L2 instruction on interlanguage pragmatic development. In N. John & L. Ortega (Eds.), *Synthesizing research on language learning and teaching* (pp. 165–211). John Benjamins.

Kang, E. Y., Sok, S., & Han, Z. (2019). Thirty-five years of ISLA on form-focused instruction: A meta-analysis. *Language Teaching Research, 23*(4), 428–453. https://doi.org/10.1177/1362168818776671

Kasper, G., & Blum-Kulka, S. (1993). Interlanguage pragmatics: An introduction. In G. Kasper & S. Blum-Kulka (Eds.), *Pragmatics in language teaching* (pp. 13–32). Cambridge University Press.

Kasper, G., & Roever, C. (2005). Pragmatics in second language learning. In E. Hinkel (Ed.), *Pragmatics in language teaching and learning* (pp. 317–328). Lawrence Erlbaum.

Kasper, G., & Rose, K. R. (1999). Pragmatics and SLA. *Annual Review of Applied Linguistics, 19*, 81–104.

Kasper, G., & Rose, K. R. (2002). Pragmatic development in a second language. *Language Learning: A Journal of Research in Language Studies, 52*(1), 1–362.

Kondo, S. (1997). The development of pragmatic competence by Japanese learners of English: Longitudinal study on interlanguage apologies. *Sophia Linguistica, 41*, 265–284.

Krashen, S. (1982). *Principles and practice in second language acquisition.* OUP.

Krulatz, A., & Dixon, T. (2020). The use of refusal strategies in interlanguage speech act performance of Korean and Norwegian users of English. *Studies in Second Language Learning and Teaching, 10*(4), 751–777.

Kubota, R., & McKay, S. (2009). Globalization and language learning in rural Japan: The role of English in the local linguistic ecology. *TESOL Quarterly, 43*(4), 593–619.

Li, S. (2010). The effectiveness of corrective feedback in SLA: A meta-analysis. *Language Learning, 60*(2), 309–365.

Li, S. (2016). The construct validity of language aptitude: A meta-analysis. *Studies in Second Language Acquisition, 38*(4), 801–842. https://doi.org/10.1017/S027226311500042X

Littlewood, W. (2014). Communication-oriented language teaching: Where are we now? Where do we go from here?. *Language Teaching, 47*(3), 349–362.

LoCastro, V. (2013). *Pragmatics for language educators: A sociolinguistic perspective.* Routledge.

References

Loewen, S. (2015). *Introduction to instructed second language acquisition*. Routledge.

Loewen, S., & Sato, M. (Eds.). (2017). *The Routledge handbook of instructed second language acquisition*. Routledge.

Long, M. H. (1996). The role of linguistic environment in second language acquisition. In W. Ritchie and T. K. Bhatia (Eds.), *Handbook of second language acquisition* (pp. 413–468). Academic Press.

MacIntyre, P. D., & Gardner, R. C. (1994). The subtle effects of language anxiety on cognitive processing in the second language. *Language Learning, 44*(2), 283–305.

Malmir, A., & Derakhshan, A. (2020). The socio-pragmatic, lexico-grammatical, and cognitive strategies in L2 pragmatic comprehension: A case of Iranian male vs. female EFL learners. *Iranian Journal of Language Teaching Research, 8*(1), 1–23. https://doi.org/10.30466/IJLTR.2020.120805

Martínez-Flor, A., & Alcón-Soler, E. (2005). Special issue: Pragmatics in instructed language learning. *System, 33*(3), 381–546.

Morris, C. W. (1938). Foundations of the theory of signs. In O. Neurath, R. Carnap, & C. W. Morris (Eds.), *International encyclopedia of unified science* (pp. 1–59). Chicago University Press.

Norrick, N. R. (1978). Expressive illocutionary acts. *Journal of Pragmatics, 2*, 277–291.

Norris, J. M., & Ortega, L. (2000). Effectiveness of L2 instruction: A research synthesis and quantitative meta-analysis. *Language Learning, 50*(3), 417–528. https://doi.org/10.1111/0023-8333.00136

Oswald, F. L., & Plonsky, L. (2010). Meta-analysis in second language research: Choices and challenges. *Annual Review of Applied Linguistics, 30*, 85–110.

Plonsky, L., & Zhuang, J. (2019). A meta-analysis of L2 pragmatics instruction. In N. Taguchi (Ed.), *The Routledge handbook of SLA and pragmatics* (pp. 287–307). Routledge.

Prabhu, N. S. (1987). *Second language pedagogy* (Vol. 20). Oxford University Press.

Reimann, A. (2011). Speech acts in foreign language acquisition. *Utsunomiya University Faculty of International Studies Research Journal, 31*(1), 67–76.

Rose, K. R. (2005). On the effects of instruction in second language pragmatics. *System, 33*(3), 385–399.

Russell, J., & Spada, N. (2006). The effectiveness of corrective feedback for the acquisition of L2 grammar: A meta-analysis of the research. In J. M. Norris & L. Ortega (Eds.), *Synthesizing research on language learning and teaching* (pp. 133–164). Benjamins.

Salazar Campillo, P. S., Safont Jordà, M. P., & Codina Espurz, V. (2009). Refusal strategies: A proposal from a sociopragmatic approach. *Asociación Española de Lingüística Aplicada, 8*, 139–150.

Sánchez-Hernández, A., & Martínez-Flor, A. (2022). Teaching the pragmatics of English as an international language: A focus on pragmatic markers. *Language Teaching Research, 26*(2), 256–278.

Schauer, G. A. (2022). Teaching pragmatics to young learners: A review study. *Applied Pragmatics, 4*(2), 137–152.

Searle, J. R. (1975). Indirect speech acts. In P. Cole & J. L. Morgan (Eds.), *Syntax and semantics* (pp. 59–82). Academic Press.

Searle, J. R. (1976). The classification of illocutionary acts. *Language in Society, 5*(1), 1–24.

Shakki, F. (2022a). Iranian EFL students' L2 engagement: The effects of teacher-student rapport and teacher support. *Language Related Research, 13*(3), 175–198. https://doi.org/10.52547/LRR.13.3.8

Shakki, F. (2022b). Meta-analysis as an emerging trend to scrutinize the effectiveness of L2 pragmatic instruction. *Frontiers in Psychology, 13*. https://doi.org/10.3389/fpsyg.2022.101666

Shakki, F., Naeini, J., Mazandarani, O., & Derakhshan, A. (2020). Instructed second language English pragmatics in the Iranian context. *Journal of Teaching Language Skills, 39*(1), 201–252. https://doi.org/10.22099/jtls.2020.38481.2886

Shakki, F., Naeini, J., Mazandarani, O., & Derakhshan, A. (2021). Instructed second language pragmatics for the speech act of apology in an Iranian EFL context: A meta-analysis. *Applied Research on English Language, 10*(3), 77–104.

Sharwood Smith, M. (1993). Input enhancement in instructed second language acquisition: Theoretical bases. *Studies in Second Language Acquisition, 15*(2), 165–180.

Schmidt, R. (1993). Consciousness, learning and interlanguage pragmatics. In G. Kasper & S. Blum-Kulka (Eds.), *Interlanguage pragmatics* (pp. 21–42). Oxford University Press.

Schmidt, R. (1995). Consciousness and foreign language learning: A tutorial on the role of attention and awareness in learning. In R. Schmidt (Ed.), *Attention and awareness in foreign language learning* (pp. 1–63). National Foreign Language Resource Center.

Schmidt, R. (2001). Attention. In P. Robinson (Ed.), *Cognition and second language instruction* (pp. 3–33). Cambridge University Press.

Skehan, P. (1998). *A cognitive approach to language learning*. Oxford University Press.

Sykes, J. M. (2009). Learner requests in Spanish: Examining the potential of multiuser virtual environments for L2 pragmatic acquisition. In L. Lomicka & G. Lord (Eds.), *The second generation: Online collaboration and social networking in CALL* (pp. 199–234). Texas State University.

Sykes, J. M., & Dubreil, S. (2019). Pragmatics learning in digital games and virtual environments. In N. Taguchi (Ed.), *The Routledge handbook of SLA and pragmatics* (pp. 387–399). Routledge.

Taguchi, N. (2011). Teaching pragmatics: Trends and issues. *Annual Review of Applied Linguistics, 31*, 289–310.

Taguchi, N. (2015). Instructed pragmatics at a glance: Where instructional studies were, are, and should be going. *Language Teaching, 48*(1), 1–50.

Taguchi, N. (Ed.). (2019). *The Routledge handbook of second language acquisition and pragmatics*. Routledge.

Taguchi, N., & Roever, C. (2017). *Second language pragmatics*. Oxford University Press.

Tajeddin, Z., & Alemi, M. (Eds.). (2020). *Pragmatics pedagogy in English as an international language*. Routledge.

Takahashi, S. (2010a). Assessing learnability in second language pragmatics. In A. Trosborg (Ed.), *Handbook of pragmatics* (pp. 391–421). Mouton de Gruyter.

Takahashi, S. (2010b). The effect of pragmatic instruction on speech act performance. In A. Martínez-Flor & E. Use-Juan (Eds.), *Speech act performance: Theoretical, empirical and methodological issues* (pp. 127–144). John Benjamins.

Takahashi, S. (2013). Awareness and learning in second language pragmatics. *Language, Culture, and Communication, 5*, 53–76.

Takahashi, S. (2015). The effects of learner profiles on pragmalinguistic awareness and learning. *System, 48*, 48–61.

van Compernolle, R. A. (2014). *Sociocultural theory and L2 instructional pragmatics*. Multilingual Matters.

Vygotsky, L. S. (1987). *Mind in society: The development of higher mental processes*. Harvard University Press.

Wang, Y., & Ren, W. (2022). The effects of proficiency and study-abroad on Chinese EFL learners' refusals. *The Language Learning Journal, 50*(4), 521–536.

Willis, D., & Willis, J. (2007). *Doing task-based teaching*. Oxford University Press.

Wilkins, D. A. (1972). *Linguistics and language teaching*. Edward Arnold.

Youn, S. J. (2018). Task design and validity evidence for assessment of L2 pragmatics in interaction. In N. Taguchi & Y. Kim (Eds.), *Task-based approaches to teaching and assessing pragmatics* (pp. 217–246). John Benjamins.

Young, R. (2011). Interactional competence in language learning, teaching, and testing. In H. Hinkel (Ed.), *Handbook of research in language learning and teaching* (pp. 426–443). Routledge.

Zangoie, A., & Derakhshan, A. (2021). Measuring the predictability of Iranian EFL students' pragmatic listening comprehension with language proficiency, self-regulated learning in listening, and willingness to communicate. *Journal of Applied Linguistics and Applied Literature: Dynamics and Advances, 9*(2), 72–104. https://doi.org/10.22049/jalda.2021.27199.1292

Zhang, Y. (2022). A mixed-methods study of computer-mediated communication paired with instruction on EFL learners' pragmatic competence. *International Journal of Computer-Assisted Language Learning and Teaching (IJCALLT), 12*(1), 1–14.

Chapter 2
Review of Previous Research

2.1 Introduction

It is pretty unanimously believed that communication would not make sense without pragmatic knowledge, and the only solution to counter this problem is pragmatic instruction (Shakki, 2022). Over the last few decades, a large body of research has considered second language pragmatics in various experimental and quasi-experimental studies. In this regard, several studies have examined the effect of different instructional methods, including input- and output-based instruction, explicit and implicit teaching, and meta-pragmatic discussion on the development of pragmatic competence (Kasper & Rose, 1999; Roever, 2009; Rose, 2005; Taguchi, 2011; Ziafar, 2020; Ziashahabi et al., 2020). Additionally, a series of review and meta-analysis papers (Derakhshan & Shakki, 2021; Jeon & Kaya, 2006; Norris & Ortega, 2000; Ren et al., 2022; Shakki et al., 2020, 2021, 2023; Taguchi, 2015; Takahashi, 2010) have been conducted regarding pragmatics instruction across various treatments, learners' factors, outcome measures, and target features by which researchers claim that instruction is more effective than just exposure to input. This chapter presents an overview of the conducted primary studies, reviews, and meta-analyses on the effectiveness of pragmatic instruction.

2.2 Recent Studies on the Instruction of the Speech Acts of Request, Apology, and Refusal

Several experimental and quasi-experimental studies have investigated the role of different instructional methods (i.e., input- and output-based instruction, explicit and implicit teaching, and meta-pragmatic discussion) on the development of pragmatic competence. Moreover, numerous studies have been conducted worldwide to check the effectiveness of teaching speech acts of request, apology, and refusal, recognized as the most frequently used speech acts (Shakki et al., 2020). More than a decade ago, Alcón-Soler and Pitarch (2010) investigated the influence of pragmatic instruction on the cognitive process for the production of refusal of translation students at a university in Spain. Ninety-two students aged 18–30 and two lecturers were involved in this study. One of the lecturers taught refusals for six weeks (two hours a week), and the other observed the classes to check for any bias pre- and post-instruction. The benefits of the pedagogical proposal during the planning and implementation of refusal and the advantages of using instruction for refusal awareness were explored in this study. The study's results indicated the importance of instruction in learner awareness, and in line with previous research, awareness-raising was proposed as an approach to teaching pragmatics. Moreover, planned pedagogical actions were found to be significant for pragmatic instruction in EFL contexts.

In another study conducted in the United Kingdom, Halenko and Jones (2011) employed six hours of explicit instruction on the speech act of request. The Chinese ESL students showed great improvement in using the request strategy after the treatment. It was found that the longer the treatment, the better the participants performed. Their results also signify the importance of explicit instruction in teaching requests in pragmatic development in a Chinese context. In a similar case, considering an Iranian context, Farrokhi and Atashian (2012) scrutinized whether explicit and implicit instruction had any effect on the comprehension and production of the speech act of refusal among 60 participants from a language institute (in explicit, implicit, and control groups) ranging in age from 19 to 25. Spectrum English book was taught to raise the pragmatic awareness of the learners. The sentence structures were explained to deduce the refusal forms in the explicit group, while in the implicit group, an input enhancement approach on sociolinguistic and pragmalinguistic factors was utilized. The efficacy of explicit instruction over implicit group was again proven in this study.

In another study by Teng and Fei (2013) conducted in a Chinese context, the speech acts of request and refusal were taken into account. The 24 participants of the explicit group were learners who received self-access material in a web-based pragmatic program utilizing contextualized strategies and appropriate language forms. Through a pretest, two groups, pre-study abroad and non-study abroad, were assessed for their pragmatic skills. Before going abroad, the experimental group received six units of instruction over about two months. After two months, a posttest was given, and the findings showed improvement in the explicit group. So, a web-based pragmatic program was suggested for the Chinese study-abroad program in order to receive the most conducive results.

Similarly, in the Iranian context, Rezvani et al. (2014) examined the role of explicit and implicit instruction on EFL students' pragmatic development in the speech acts of suggestions and requests. They selected 60 intermediate EFL students from a language institute and divided them into two main groups: implicit and explicit. To check the participants' ability to use the speech acts of suggestions and requests, the researchers distributed a pretest among the participants. Then, the implicit and explicit groups were shown recordings of short dialogues. The results of the posttest, administered after the treatment, demonstrated that both implicit and explicit instruction greatly impacted the students' pragmatic competence, though the explicit group outperformed its implicit counterpart.

Considering the role of task-based instruction and its complexity, Kim and Taguchi (2015) employed a six-week treatment among 73 Korean junior high school students. A Discourse Completion Test (DCT) was used to measure the oral interaction of the learners during the tasks. The findings revealed that task complexity levels influenced the production of requests; however, there was no difference between the simple and complex tasks. Another study conducted in an Iranian context by Rajabi et al. (2015) investigated the impact of explicit instruction on the pragmatic development of language learners. They randomly assigned 73 intermediate students from four EFL classes into the experimental and control group. Prior to treatment, a DCT was administered as a pretest to assess the students' pragmatic competence. Then, the experimental group received instruction on the speech act of apology for half an hour. A posttest was then given to the students to measure the effect of instruction. The results of the posttest indicated that explicit instruction greatly influenced students' pragmatic competence.

In the USA, Cunningham's investigation (2016), part of Cunningham's more extensive 2014 study, was carried out for the course "German for Professions," in which the learners experience German business culture through engaging in appropriate content. Speech act production for expressing requests by American learners of German while they were interacting with German-speaking professionals in Germany was checked via synchronous web conferences. The implementation of focused instruction and interaction with expert speakers was analyzed through quantitative and qualitative methods, and it was found that instruction and telecollaboration can lead to measurable gains of pragmatic competence.

Regarding the immediate effect of pragmatic instruction, Alcón-Soler (2017) examined emails produced by 60 Spanish learners. The learners who were studying in England were checked for the frequency of indirect request strategies and internal modifiers. The results accentuated the importance of instruction and its significant effect on producing requests. Another study was conducted by Gazioglu and Çiftci (2017), who examined the effect of instruction on the speech act of request on Turkish learners of English in a Turkish context. The students' comprehension was explored in their pragmatic classes. Twenty-six learners, including 16 males and 10 females, in the 9th grade in a state high school in Turkey participated in this study. A DCT with eight situations was used for both the pretest and posttest to check the effectiveness of instruction. In addition to the DCT, student papers, a survey, and researchers' notes were also used to run the analysis. Interestingly, the study results indicated no significant difference between the pre and posttest. However, a variety of structures and strategies were used by the participants after the posttest.

Using Martínez-Flor and Usó-Juan's (2006) approach, Purwanti (2018) also carried out research on 34 undergraduate students in Indonesia to see whether pragmatic instruction changed the English requests production for Indonesians. The posttest results were compared with the pretest, revealing an improvement in request production. It was reported that the students sometimes used lexical, phrasal, and internal modifications after the treatment. In a similar vein, Derakhshan and Arabmofrad (2018) investigated the effect of video-enhanced input on the comprehension of three speech acts of apology, request, and refusal of 69 Iranian EFL students. There were four groups, form-search, interactive translation, metapragmatic, and control, in which the participants were randomly distributed. The participants were analyzed after watching 60 video vignettes extracted from various episodes of Friends and Seinfeld sitcoms. It was reported that the metapragmatic approach most improved the pragmatic comprehension of the consciousness-raising, interactive translation, and form-search groups. Similar to the previous findings, this study supported the importance of pragmatic instruction.

In the Thai context, Omanee and Krishnasamy (2019) examined the production of requests of hospitality undergraduates making polite requests for hotel front office service by using YouTube instructions. The participants were 30 students from the Rajamangala University of Technology Srivijayan in Thailand in their third year of a hospitality degree. Receptionist and guest conversation clips, movie fragment clips, and a set of request tutorials make up the material for a seven-and-a-half-hour treatment over five weeks. Five stages of instruction, form search, form comparison, form analysis, practice, and discussion, were used. A DCT was used for data collection, and the data was interpreted through descriptive analysis and t-test. The results had a significant and positive effect on request instruction using a YouTube intervention teaching model.

Considering the speech act of apology in the context of Iraq, Shark (2019) conducted a study in which the effect of explicit and implicit instruction on advanced EFL learners' pragmatic knowledge was checked. The participants were 40 Iraqi Kurdish EFL learners studying in the 12th grade at the British International School in Erbil, Iraq. First, their proficiency level was checked using an Oxford Quick Placement Test (OQPT), then they were randomly divided into two groups, implicit and explicit instruction. Several different examples of real-life apology situations were given to the learners through an MDCT as a pretest. Ten native English speakers were also given the same test to provide appropriate answers for comparison. After the intervention, the same test was again given to the participants, and the findings revealed that both explicit and implicit groups improved, though the explicit group outperformed its implicit counterpart. Both groups demonstrated significant effects of instruction in both the posttest and the delayed posttest. Moreover, when the results were compared with the findings of English native speakers' tests, all groups differed in choosing the most appropriate answers in different situations.

Similarly, Derakhshan and Shakki (2020) investigated the impact of implicit and explicit metapragmatic instruction on Iranian EFL students' pragmatic comprehension of two speech acts: apology and refusal. After running an Oxford Quick Placement Test (2004), 49 EFL students from a state university were chosen to participate in this study. They were assigned into three groups implicit, explicit, and control. They employed a validated DCT with 128 items (8 conversations for the speech act of refusal and 8 for the speech act of apology). A one-way ANOVA revealed that students' pragmatic comprehension across the two treatment groups improved after the treatment. The findings accentuated the importance of instruction for the mentioned speech acts in a foreign language context. By the same token, Ziashahabi et al. (2020) examined the effects of instruction of English conversational implicatures on the development of EFL students' pragmatic competence. To this end, 63 EFL learners were chosen and randomly assigned into experimental and control groups. To gather data on the identification of conversational implicatures, the researchers administered a 20-item test to the participants. Employing one-way between-groups analysis of covariance (ANCOVA), they found that EFL students' pragmatic competence improved drastically as a result of instruction.

Subsequently, Ziafar (2020) explored the effect of implicit, explicit, and contrastive lexical approaches on EFL students' pragmatic competence. To do so, 63 EFL students were chosen and divided into three treatment groups. Several episodes of a TV sitcom were selected as the primary source of pragmatic instruction. The posttest findings revealed that instruction notably improved all students' pragmatic competence. In the context of the Philippines, Alaga-Acosta (2020) investigated the speech acts performed by student participants in society. Eight situations were given to the learners in a discourse completion oral test, and they were asked to perform them through a role-play presentation. The student participants did not know they were in a research project, and their real-life performances were recorded. The results indicated that the student participants preferred to use directive speech acts in terms of requesting, particularly for performative, imperative, and personal needs. Interestingly, the students did not contain their emotions and had limited use of polite words. The number of indirect words and hedges used by the learners was smaller than expected. Moreover, students did not successfully mitigate directness, which corroborates the importance of instruction in EFL classes.

Taking task-based instruction and pragmatics into consideration, Zand-Moghadam and Samani (2021) selected 60 intermediate EFL learners (33 females and 27 males) in their study. The participants, ranging in age from 16 to 46, were selected from a private language institute in Tehran. The *American English File* series was used to teach the learners. A written Discourse Completion Task (WDCT), metapragmatic awareness questionnaire, implicature comprehension test, and some instructional materials were among the instruments used in this study. The positive effects of task-based instruction were highlighted when they taught the speech acts of request, apology, and refusal to twenty members of three groups through opinion-gap, information-gap, and reasoning-gap tasks. The findings showed that the learners in the information-gap task group outperformed the other learners, and production and metapragmatic awareness resulted from instruction.

Bouftira et al. (2022) conducted a quasi-experimental study exploring the use of a blended learning model in teaching pragmatics. Sixty-two junior high school students participated in this research, and their level of pragmatic competence was evaluated at the end of the study. The results showed that the blended learning model led to a significant increase in pragmatic competence, and the experimental group outperformed the control group. This study also highly recommended using foreign language teachers to enhance pragmatic awareness in their classes. Moreover, Myrset (2022) scrutinized the effect of concept-based instruction of request in a primary school in Norway. Two groups consisting of 7th-grade students whose age was around 12 were selected to participate in this study. Some external strategies and sociopragmatic dimensions of requests were taught to the learners before the posttest, consisting of a video-prompted oral DCT. The results showed an increased use of modal verbs and variation in producing the speech act of request.

Quite recently, Usó-Juan (2022) explored the effect of explicit strategy instruction to write email requests to faculty of Spanish learners. Taking Taguchi's (2018) classification into account, the treatment was carried out to allow the learners to perceive the form-function-context mapping of email requests in their context. One hundred ten email requests were received both before the treatment and after engaging the learners in the learning process at two different times. The emails were analyzed based on their appropriateness and variety of structures. The findings showed that more appropriate emails were written by the group which received instruction. The results suggested that pragmatic instruction leads to pragmatic development.

Having reviewed the existing literature on the role of pragmatic instruction for speech acts of request, apology, and refusal, it should be noted that the majority of these studies were mainly confined to mere instruction. Therefore, it is a challenge to determine whether the overall effectiveness of instruction has been confirmed and if so, whether there are any factors and moderators which can predict this effectiveness. In this regard, researchers commenced writing reviews and meta-analyses to pave the way to find the answers to these questions.

2.3 Previous Reviews and Meta-Analyses in L2 Pragmatic

Although some research attention has recently been given to the instruction of pragmatics, conducting reviews and meta-analyses in this field is still in its infancy. Investigation into the effectiveness of instruction was started after Kasper's (1996) plenary talk, and these studies have inspired a couple of reviews and meta-analyses on instructed pragmatics. More particularly on the concept of instruction, Norris and Ortega (2000) scrutinized papers published over 18 years from 1980 to 1998. They found 49 samples which include sufficient data to be used in their study. They found that focused L2 instruction and explicit groups are more effective than other counterparts since they result in more language learning. Their findings revealed that both focus on form and focus on forms lead to significant effects. Their study was among the first meta-analyses on the effectiveness of L2 instruction, reporting an effect size of $d = 0.96$ which is quite large and corroborates the overall effectiveness of instruction. Since effect sizes of $d = 0.80$ or greater can be considered large effects (Cohen, 1988), Norris and Ortega's (2002) results for focus on form ($d = 1.00$), focus on forms ($d = 0.93$), explicit ($d = 1.13$), and implicit treatments ($d = 0.54$) made it clear that explicit instruction generated greater effects than implicit instruction. With these results in mind, the study reported this pattern: Focus on form explicit > focus on forms explicit > focus on form implicit > focus on forms implicit. They proposed that researchers focus on other aspects of instruction in their further studies.

2.3 Previous Reviews and Meta-Analyses in L2 Pragmatic

The first meta-analysis on L2 pragmatics instruction was conducted about 16 years ago by Jeon and Kaya (2006), using 13 studies published prior to 2003. The overall effect they found for the effectiveness of pragmatic instruction was $d = 1.57$, which was large and significant. They reported the superiority of explicit over implicit instruction by generating the effects $d = 0.70$ for explicit and $d = 0.44$ for implicit instruction between groups. Moreover, they found that longer treatments (more than five hours of instruction) yielded larger effect sizes than short-term interventions. Considering the outcome measures of two categories, receptive tasks (multiple-choice tests) and productive tasks (written or oral DCT and role play), their findings represent a larger effect size for productive tasks than multiple-choice tests. Since they utilized a small sample size, other research and additional evidence were suggested to corroborate their findings. Jeon and Kaya's (2006) study contained six studies targeting speech acts such as the request and seven studies targeting a mixture of sociopragmatic features, syntactic-semantic structure, and implicatures. However, they did not focus on the speech acts in isolation, and further research is required to provide more accurate claims regarding the type of speech acts and the effectiveness of pragmatic instruction.

Following Jeon and Kaya (2006), Takahashi (2010) reviewed 49 studies on pragmatic instruction. In her review, she highlighted the effect of explicit instruction over non-instruction or implicit teaching; however, she also reported reasons why explicit instruction alone is not entirely acceptable. She believes that since both positive and negative results are reported for explicit interventions and because these interventions do not allow learners to become substantially confident in performing the speech acts, they cannot be as promising as they seem. Thus, providing meta-pragmatic information is suggested to increase the teachability of pragmatics through interventions. She found that implicit teaching can be effective by leading the learners to pragmatic rules while directing their attention to pragmatic features. Furthermore, she explained two vital factors in promoting pragmatic instruction: higher proficiency levels and motivation. She explained the importance of intrinsic motivation, which can change the learners' attitude toward pragmatic development, and suggested that teachers focus on some attributable variables of the learners to achieve the best results. Another review article by Taguchi (2015) on the development of instructed pragmatics over the past three decades used 58 instructional intervention studies based on which instruction is believed to be more beneficial than non-instruction for her review. She claimed that explicit teaching is typically more effective than implicit, though implicit teaching can be conducive if it involves activities on noticing and processing. Regarding the outcome measures, Taguchi (2015) found that role-play as a measure can check the pragmalinguistic knowledge of the learners in negotiations and interactions, but DCTs better measure the learners' knowledge and competence of pragmalinguistic forms. She found that the effectiveness of instruction can vary from large to small based on the method of assessing the treatments and outcome measures. Therefore, this factor is also pivotal and needs to be scrutinized. Her review paper also needs to be updated to consider variations and stability in the findings.

Similarly, to Jeon and Kaya (2006), Badjadi (2016) utilized 24 studies to find the differentiated effects of second language pragmatics' instructional methods and outcome measures, namely, comprehension, structured production, and free production. One of the criticisms leveled against this meta-analysis was that only two moderator variables were investigated as opposed to the many moderators in previous reviews and meta-analyses (Plonsky & Zhuang, 2019). They found that instruction with feedback is more effective than teaching without feedback. The effect size generated for explicit instruction in his study was $d = 1.96$ compared to implicit instruction of $d = 1.01$. Although the explicit group yielded a larger effect size across all outcome measures, implicit instruction produced a larger effect size with comprehension tasks. These findings revealed that production and comprehension mean effect sizes change from small to large, similar to instructional tasks. Since only two moderator variables were scrutinized and many primary studies published in this field were excluded from this study, the results of this meta-analysis have come under question, and its comprehensiveness was reduced; hence other research and meta-analyses were recommended.

Subsequently, Plonsky and Zhuang (2019) raised some research questions concerning the overall effectiveness of pragmatic instruction and the variables which can moderate this effectiveness. Their study focused on contextual and learner factors, treatment and target features, outcome measures, and research and reporting practices. The results lend support to the previous meta-analyses in which the importance of explicit instruction was accentuated over its implicit counterpart. They found the effect of $d = 1.52$ for the overall effectiveness of pragmatic instruction, which is quite large and confirmed the teachability of pragmatics. Taking the second research question into account, interestingly, their results displayed larger effect sizes in language institutes and high schools than in universities. More importantly, larger gains were shown in highly proficient learners than in learners at lower proficiency levels. The next variable, the treatment method, generated a large effect size for the following four instructional features: feedback, the opportunity for practice, enhanced input, and metapragmatic information. Conversely, the consciousness-raising treatment method yielded a relatively small effect size of $d = 0.11$ and $d = 0.12$ for explicit and implicit instruction, respectively. Another variable taken into account was the length of study, which was operationalized in different ways by the previous studies and meta-analyses (less/more than 5 weeks in Jeon and Kaya [2006]; less/more than two weeks in Plonsky [2011]; and less/more than 4.25 weeks in Lee et al. [2015]). This moderator was reported to generate a relatively small correlation for both groups of the study, $d = 0.21, 0.23$. Regarding the outcome measures, the larger effects were generated by productive skills, such as role plays and written DCTs, than the receptive skills, such as multiple-choices and DCTs. Plonsky and Zhuang (2019) recommend that researchers explore the foreign language context rather than the second language context. They also stressed that researchers should report research designs and data analysis, issues which were taken into account in this study.

Similarly, Yousefi and Nassaji (2019) investigated the effects of instruction on L2 pragmatics in 39 published studies from 2006 to 2016. In addition to the previous meta-analyses' focus on the overall effectiveness of pragmatic instruction and the moderator variables, they aimed to study the effect of face-to-face versus computer-mediated instruction and added the proficiency level to the analyzed variables. Similar

2.3 Previous Reviews and Meta-Analyses in L2 Pragmatic

to the prior studies, they reported a large effect size of $d = 1.10$ for the overall effectiveness of pragmatics. With respect to the instructional mode, computer-mediated produced a larger effect of $d = 1.17$ than face-to-face instruction with $d = 0.96$. Moreover, explicit instruction yielded larger effects ($d = 1.21$) than implicit instruction ($d = 0.87$). Most importantly, instruction was found more effective for comprehension ($d = 1.34$) than production ($d = 1.06$).

Interestingly, contrary to Jeon and Kaya (2006) and Plonsky and Zhuang (2019), they found a larger effect in the comprehension of more constrained responses, such as multiple-choice DCTs ($d = 1.12$), than response production ($d = 0.95$) in comparison to productive tasks such as role plays and descriptions ($d = 0.70$). Furthermore, their results illustrated larger effect sizes for long ($d = 1.55$) and medium ($d = 1.47$) hours of treatment than short hours ($d = 0.75$). The proficiency level, coded as beginner, intermediate, and advanced learners, produced $d = 0.76$, $d = 1.13$, and $d = 0.83$ effect sizes, respectively. It is clear that the intermediate group benefited more than the other two groups. Last but not least, the study checked the durability of the results. They reported $d = 1.08$ for an immediate posttest and $d = 0.93$ for a delayed posttest, highlighting the importance of conducting immediate posttests. As mentioned in their limitations, they did not analyze specific pragmatic features such as speech acts, nor did they take into account learners' factors, and they recommend conducting research based on the new moderator variables and pragmatic features.

In an Iranian review, Shakki et al. (2020) analyzed studies on the instruction of pragmatics. They found 54 studies on the instruction of pragmatic speech acts. Among them, the speech act of request was recognized as the most frequent speech act in 29 studies, apology was the second most common speech act in 26 studies, refusal in 11 studies, suggestion, complaint, and compliment followed in four studies apiece, and thanking in two studies. Interestingly, the speech act of invitation received scant attention, with only one study in an Iranian context. Various methods of assessment of pragmatics were utilized in the published papers, with the Multiple Discourse Completion Test (MDCT) being the most dominant in 36 studies, closely followed by the Written Discourse Completion Test (WDCT) in 19 studies; there were also 13 papers that used both (MDCT and WDCT). Other studies, such as Eslami and Mardani (2010), utilized different data collection methods, such as diagnostic assessments or DCTs. Shakki et al. also scrutinized different treatment types used to teach non-native students. They reported 25 studies with explicit vs. implicit and control groups, 30 with explicit vs. control types, and 30 with a variety of treatments such as dictogloss, consciousness-raising, interactive translation, etc. Regarding the research designs, 42 out of 54 studies used the pretest, posttest vs. control design, while the rest utilized the pretest vs. posttest design. Only one study was found to use a qualitative design (Tajeddin & Hosseinpur, 2014a, 2014b). What they found was a general picture of the instruction of pragmatic speech acts among Iranian students and they proposed conducting other meta-analyses to check the effectiveness of instruction and to identify the moderators.

Moreover, Derakhshan and Shakki (2021) conducted a meta-analysis on the effectiveness of the instruction of the speech act of request in the Iranian context. After analyzing 37 studies on the instruction of request, based on special inclusion/

exclusion criteria, they selected 17 primary studies. The analysis of their first research question concerning the overall effectiveness of request instruction generated a large effect size of $g = 1.20$. Taking the moderators into consideration, participants' age was coded as 10–20, 20–30, and mixed in their study. It was found that for learners between 10 and 20 years, the effect size was $g = 2.14$, for those from 20 to 30 ($g = 1.50$), and for the mixed group ($g = 0.63$). Since the results of meta-regression were not significant, they found age was not among the predictors of instruction effectiveness in their study. Another moderator used in their paper was gender, coded as male, female, mixed, and not reported group. The following effect sizes were obtained for each of the mentioned groups: male ($g = 3.09$), female ($g = 1.10$), mixed ($g = 1.25$), and not reported ($g = 1.84$). Interestingly, gender was found to be a predictor variable for the instruction of pragmatics, especially the speech act of request. Proficiency level was also a variable analyzed in their meta-analysis. Regarding elementary learners, the effect size generated was $g = 0.67$, for the intermediate group ($g = 1.57$), upper-intermediate ($g = 2.14$), advanced learners ($g = 1.69$), and the not reported group ($g = 1.41$). Except for the elementary group, other proficiency levels produced large and significant effect sizes. The next variable used in this study was the research design with the effect sizes of ($g = 1.72$) for the experimental group and ($g = 1.40$) for the quasi-experimental group. While both were positive and large, they were not significant enough to be a predictor for this effectiveness. This study also analyzed treatment type, and the explicit group generated a larger effect size ($g = 1.53$) than the implicit counterpart ($g = 1.20$). It was also found that treatment type can be another predictor for the instruction of request. Moreover, the last factor analyzed in this study was the outcome measure. Three types of measurements, MDCT ($g = 1.58$), WDCT ($g = 1.47$), and mixed methods ($g = 1.43$), were found to be positive and large regarding their effect sizes. The researchers analyzed the request speech act in their study, and other meta-analyses on other speech acts were proposed for further study.

In the same vein, Shakki et al. (2021) conducted another meta-analysis on the effectiveness of apology instruction in an Iranian context using 12 studies selected based on special exclusion and inclusion criteria from 31 primary studies. The overall effect they found for pragmatic instruction of apology was $g = 1.34$, which was medium and positive. They also investigated whether treatment types and research designs can be predictor variables that moderate the effectiveness of pragmatic instruction. Considering the treatment types, the authors coded explicit and implicit groups for teaching apologies, with the following effects generated based on the analyses, $g = 1.25$ and $g = 1.44$, respectively. Interestingly, the effect size for implicit instruction of apology was much larger than explicit teaching, which shows the positive and significant impact of implicit instruction. Considering research design as another variable, the experimental group yielded the effect of $g = 0.92$, while the quasi-experimental group displayed a positive and large effect ($g = 2.39$). Moreover, the research design was considered as a predictor for apology instruction. Finally, this study focused on the speech act of apology, and it proposed that researchers focus on other speech acts.

2.3 Previous Reviews and Meta-Analyses in L2 Pragmatic

Similarly, Ren et al. (2022) ran a meta-analysis to check the effectiveness of pragmatic instruction. Out of 958 items, they selected the studies using a between-group design, with the defined dependent variable of learners' performance. After considering the inclusion and exclusion criteria, 54 studies were included in their analysis. Their coding schema consisted of (1) research settings, whether it is a foreign or second language context; (2) institutional level, whether they are a learner at a university, language institute, high school, or pre-high school; (3) teaching approaches, explicit or implicit; (4) treatment length, defined as less or more than three hours and considered as long, medium, or short; (5) pragmatic target, if they are speech acts or routines; (6) learners' language proficiency, whether they are at an advance, intermediate, novice, or unspecified level; (7) target language, English or other languages; (8) outcome measures, whether they are WDCTs, oral productional tasks, or multiple-choice task; and (9) pragmatic sub-competence, if they are production or perception. The effect size they reported for their first research question was $g = 1.65$, which indicates a large and significant effect for teaching pragmatic features. With regard to the research setting, the effect for learners in the foreign context was rather larger ($g = 2.12$) than in the second language ($g = 0.73$). Furthermore, the learners in high school yielded a larger effect size ($g = 4.47$) than the pre-high school participants ($g = 1.04$). Similar to other meta-analyses, the explicit group performed slightly better ($g = 1.73$) than the implicit group ($g = 1.51$). Regarding the length of treatments, the long treatment (more than 18 h) produced a larger effect size ($g = 3.48$) than the medium ($g = 1.62$) treatment (between 3 and 18 h), and the short-time treatment (less than 3 h) generated a quite small effect size ($g = 0.87$). Analyzing the pragmatic targets, speech acts yielded a larger effect size ($g = 1.69$) than routines, but the results may be related to the number of studies done on the routines. In checking the proficiency levels, most studies included intermediate learners with an effect of $g = 1.81$; the advanced level generated a larger effect size ($g = 0.84$) than novice groups ($g = 0.59$). Moreover, those who used English as a target language produced a larger effect size ($g = 1.86$) than other languages ($g = 0.85$). Investigating the outcome measures, WDCTs yielded the largest effect size ($g = 2.08$), followed by oral tasks such as role-play ($g = 1.50$) and multiple tasks ($g = 0.94$). Considering the last moderator of pragmatic sub-competence, production generated a smaller effect ($g = 1.54$) than perception ($g = 1.99$). Overall, they recommended that researchers continue to work on other moderators that affect pragmatic instruction.

In another recent Iranian meta-analysis, Shakki et al. (2023) studied the effectiveness of instruction for the three dominant speech acts: request, apology, and refusal. After a thorough search among 80 primary studies, 98 effect sizes were extracted from 57 final studies. The effect size of $g = 1.43$ was reported for the effectiveness of pragmatic instruction of request, apology, and refusal, which reflects a large gain in teaching efficacy. More specifically, they found 23 studies on request, 18 on apology, and five on refusal. In these studies, 32 utilized explicit instruction, ten implicit, and eight, a mixture of explicit and implicit. In addition, most of the studies involved intermediate language level participants older than 18. Finally, the authors also proposed conducting meta-analyses in other contexts with other variables.

2.4 Conclusion

Reviewing the previous meta-analyses on the effectiveness of pragmatic instruction reveals that there has been no meta-analysis on the effectiveness of L2 pragmatic instruction in which the speech acts of request, apology, and refusal are scrutinized worldwide. The meta-analyses undertaken by researchers during the last decades present only a small sample of the conducted research. In some cases, like Ren et al. (2022), the inclusion and exclusion of the data were so limited that most of the studies were removed from the corpus. Because their dependent variable was the learners' performance and they selected between-group design studies, their findings were not comprehensive enough. Other studies like Shakki et al. (2021) or Derakhshan and Shakki (2021) were conducted on just one speech act, while others have been ignored in their research. Moreover, the number of primary studies is too limited in some studies like Jeon and Kaya (2006) or Yousefi and Nassaji (2019). Considering the shortcomings of the previous meta-analyses, the present book aimed to check the effectiveness of L2 pragmatics instruction in the case of request, apology, and refusal in papers published between 2000 and 2022.

References

Alaga-Acosta, N. A. (2020). Speech acts analysis among second language learners: Basis for an enhanced English as second language (ESL) instruction on pragmatics. *Journal of Academic Research, 5*(3), 28–38.

Alcón-Soler, E. (2017). Pragmatic development during study abroad: An analysis of Spanish teenagers' request strategies in English emails. *Annual Review of Applied Linguistics, 37*, 77–92.

Alcón-Soler, E., & Pitarch, J. G. (2010). The effect of instruction on learners' pragmatic awareness: A focus on refusals. *International Journal of English Studies, 10*(1), 65–80.

Badjadi, N. E. I. (2016). A meta-analysis of the effects of instructional tasks on L2 pragmatics comprehension and production. In S. F. Tang & L. Logonnathan (Eds.), *Assessment for learning within and beyond the classroom* (pp. 241–268). Springer.

Bouftira, M., El Messaoudi, M., & Li, S. (2022). Developing EFL learners' pragmatic competence through a blended learning model: A quasi-experimental study. *European Scientific Journal (ESJ), 18*(16), 105–132. https://doi.org/10.19044/esj.2022.v18n16p105

Cunningham, D. J. (2016). Request modification in synchronous computer-mediated communication: The role of focused instruction. *The Modern Language Journal, 100*(2), 484–507.

Cohen, J. (1988). *Statistical power analysis for the behavioral sciences* (2nd ed.). Hillsdale.

Derakhshan, A., & Arabmofrad, A. (2018). The impact of instruction on the pragmatic comprehension of speech acts of apology, request, and refusal among Iranian intermediate EFL learners. *English Teaching & Learning, 42*(1), 75–94.

Derakhshan, A., & Shakki, F. (2020). The effect of implicit vs. explicit metapragmatic instruction on the Iranian intermediate EFL learners' pragmatic comprehension of apology and refusal. *Journal of Language Research, 12*(37), 151–175.

Derakhshan, A., & Shakki, F. (2021). A meta-analytic study of instructed second language pragmatics: A case of the speech act of request. *Journal of Research in Applied Linguistics, 12*(1), 15–32. https://doi.org/10.22055/RALS.2021.16722

References

Eslami-Rasekh, A., & Mardani, M. (2010). Investigating the effects of teaching apology speech act, with a focus on intensifying strategies, on pragmatic development of EFL learners: The Iranian context. *The International Journal of Language Society and Culture, 30*(1), 96–103.

Farrokhi, F., & Atashian, S. (2012). The role of refusal instruction in pragmatic development. *World Journal of Education, 2*(4), 85–93.

Gazioglu, T., & Çiftci, H. (2017). Developing pragmatic competence through teaching requests in English classrooms. *Journal of Uludağ University Faculty of Education, 30*(1), 139–165.

Halenko, N., & Jones, C. (2011). Teaching pragmatic awareness of spoken requests to Chinese EAP learners in the UK: Is explicit instruction effective? *System, 39*(2), 240–250.

Jeon, E. H., & Kaya, T. (2006). Effects of L2 instruction on interlanguage pragmatic development. In N. John & L. Ortega (Eds.), *Synthesizing research on language learning and teaching* (pp. 165–211). John Benjamins.

Kasper, G. (1996). Introduction: Interlanguage pragmatics in SLA. *Studies in Second Language Acquisition, 18*(2), 145–148.

Kasper, G., & Rose, K. R. (1999). Pragmatics and SLA. *Annual Review of Applied Linguistics, 19*, 81–104.

Kim, Y., & Taguchi, N. (2015). Promoting task-based pragmatics instruction in EFL classroom contexts: The role of task complexity. *The Modern Language Journal, 99*(4), 656–677.

Martínez-Flor, A., & Usó-Juan, E. (2006). A comprehensive pedagogical framework to develop pragmatics in the foreign language classroom: The 6Rs approach. *Applied Language Learning, 16*(2), 39–63.

Myrset, A. (2022). 'You could win Masterchef with this soup. Can I get some more?' Request production and the impact of instruction on young EFL learners. *Journal of Pragmatics, 192*, 56–76.

Norris, J. M., & Ortega, L. (2000). Effectiveness of L2 instruction: A research synthesis and quantitative meta-analysis. *Language Learning, 50*(3), 417–528. https://doi.org/10.1111/0023-8333.00136

Omanee, B., & Krishnasamy, H. N. (2019). Pragmatic development of Thai EFL hospitality undergraduates through YouTube intervention instruction: A case of the speech act of request at hotel front desk service. *Journal of Applied Linguistics and Language Research, 6*(5), 79–94.

Plonsky, L. (2011). The effectiveness of second language strategy instruction: A meta-analysis. *Language Learning, 61*(4), 993–1038.

Plonsky, L., & Zhuang, J. (2019). A meta-analysis of L2 pragmatics instruction. In N. Taguchi (Ed.), *The Routledge handbook of SLA and pragmatics* (pp. 287–307). Routledge.

Purwanti, I. T. (2018). *Pragmatic instruction effects on students' EFL production: A qualitative analysis*. Proceedings of the UR International Conference on Educational Sciences, Pekanbaru, Indonesia, 48–55.

Rajabi, S., Azizifar, A., & Gowhary, H. (2015). Investigating the explicit instruction of apology speech act on pragmatic development of Iranian EFL learners. *Advances in Language and Literary Studies, 6*(4), 53–61.

Ren, W., Li, S., & Lü, X. (2022). A meta-analysis of the effectiveness of second language pragmatics instruction. *Applied Linguistics*, 1–21. https://doi.org/10.1093/applin/amac055

Rezvani, E., Eslami-Rasekh, A., & Vahid Dastjerdi, H. (2014). Investigating the effects of explicit and implicit instruction on Iranian EFL learners' pragmatic development: Speech acts of request and suggestion in focus. *International Journal of Research Studies in Language Learning, 3*(7), 1–12.

Roever, C. (2009). Teaching and testing pragmatics. In M. H. Long & C. J. Doughty (Eds.), *The handbook of language teaching* (pp. 560–577). Wiley-Blackwell.

Rose, K. R. (2005). On the effects of instruction in second language pragmatics. *System, 33*(3), 385–399.

Shakki, F. (2022). Iranian EFL students' L2 engagement: The effects of teacher-student rapport and teacher support. *Language Related Research, 13*(3), 175–198.

Shakki, F., Naeini, J., Mazandarani, O., & Derakhshan, A. (2020). Instructed second language English pragmatics in the Iranian context. *Journal of Teaching Language Skills, 39*(1), 201–252. https://doi.org/10.22099/jtls.2020.38481.2886

Shakki, F., Naeini, J., Mazandarani, O., & Derakhshan, A. (2021). Instructed second language pragmatics for the speech act of apology in an Iranian EFL context: A meta-analysis. *Applied Research on English Language, 10*(3), 77–104.

Shakki, F., Neaini, J., Mazandarani, O., & Derakhshan, A. (2023). A meta-analysis on the instructed second language pragmatics for the speech acts of apology, request, and refusal in an Iranian EFL context. *Language Related Research, 13*(6), 461–510.

Shark, P. (2019). The effects of explicit/implicit instructions on the development of advanced EFL learners' pragmatic knowledge of English: Apology speech act. *Journal of Language Teaching and Research, 10*(1), 76–82.

Taguchi, N. (2011). Teaching pragmatics: Trends and issues. *Annual Review of Applied Linguistics, 31*, 289–310.

Taguchi, N. (2015). Instructed pragmatics at a glance: Where instructional studies were, are, and should be going. *Language Teaching, 48*(1), 1–50.

Taguchi, N. (2018). Contexts and pragmatics learning: Problems and opportunities of the study abroad research. *Language Teaching, 51*(1), 124–137.

Tajeddin, Z., & Hosseinpur, R. (2014a). The impact of deductive, inductive, and L1-based consciousness-raising tasks on EFL learners' acquisition of the request speech act. *Journal of Teaching Language Skills, 33*(1), 73–92.

Tajeddin, Z., & Hosseinpur, R. M. (2014b). The role of consciousness-raising tasks on EFL learners' microgenetic development of request pragmatic knowledge. *Iranian Journal of Applied Linguistics (IJAL), 17*(1), 147–187.

Takahashi, S. (2010). The effect of pragmatic instruction on speech act performance. In A. Martínez-Flor & E. Use-Juan (Eds.), *Speech act performance: Theoretical, empirical and methodological issues* (pp. 127–144). John Benjamins.

Teng, C., & Fei, F. (2013). A consciousness-raising approach to pragmatics teaching: Web-based tasks for training study-abroad students. *Journal of Technology and Chinese Language Teaching, 4*(1), 50–63.

Usó-Juan, E. (2022). Exploring the role of strategy instruction on learners' ability to write authentic email requests to faculty. *Language Teaching Research, 26*(2), 213–237.

Yousefi, M., & Nassaji, H. (2019). A meta-analysis of the effects of instruction and corrective feedback on L2 pragmatics and the role of moderator variables: Face-to-face vs. computer-mediated instruction. *ITL-International Journal of Applied Linguistics, 170*(2), 277–308. https://doi.org/10.1075/itl.19012.you

Zand-Moghadam, A., & Samani, F. M. (2021). Effect of information-gap, reasoning-gap, and opinion-gap tasks on EFL learners' pragmatic production, metapragmatic awareness, and comprehension of implicature. *TESL-EJ, 25*(1).

Ziafar, M. (2020). The influence of explicit, implicit, and contrastive lexical approaches on pragmatic competence: The case of Iranian EFL learners. *International Review of Applied Linguistics in Language Teaching, 58*(1), 103–131.

Ziashahabi, S., Jabbari, A. A., & Razmi, M. H. (2020). The effect of interventionist instructions of English conversational implicatures on Iranian EFL intermediate level learners' pragmatic competence development. *Cogent Education, 7*(1), 1–20. https://doi.org/10.1080/2331186X.2020.1840008

Chapter 3
Methodology

3.1 Introduction

Studies on pragmatic instruction have been carried out on various speech acts in different contexts over the last decades (Shakki, 2022). Among the speech acts, request, apology, and refusal are considered the most frequent and valued (Shakki et al., 2020). The purpose of the study reported in the present chapter is twofold: first, it aims to unravel the overall effectiveness of pragmatic instruction for the speech acts of request, apology, and refusal; and second, it is intended to scrutinize whether different variables such as age, gender, proficiency level, treatment types, outcome measures, research design, psycholinguistic features, and speech act types moderate this effectiveness. Finally, this chapter elaborates on the research design, the study selection process from various journals and databases, the coding protocol by which the studies were categorized, the missing data, reliability, and the bias which may exist in publications.

3.2 Research Questions

The following research questions were formulated to scrutinize the effectiveness of L2 pragmatic instruction on the speech acts of request, apology, and refusal:

1. What is the overall effectiveness of the instruction of L2 pragmatics, particularly the speech acts of request, apology, and refusal?
2. What are the variables that moderate the effectiveness of L2 pragmatic instruction, especially the speech acts of request, apology, and refusal?

3.3 Research Design

Meta-analysis is not a formal experimental study and can be considered non-experimental or descriptive research. It is a formal, and quantitative study design utilized to systematically assess previous studies' findings to obtain conclusions about that specific concept in a body of research (Glass, 1976; Plonsky & Gass, 2011; Plonsky & Oswald, 2014). Meta-analyses involve thorough search patterns that enable researchers to identify pertinent studies on a particular topic (DeLuca et al., 2008). It also allows researchers to synthesize the outcomes quantitatively to get statistical significance and relevant data. It can potentially extend data-rich databases, leading to more secondary analyses. To collect the available studies comprehensively, search strategies and criteria must be sensitive enough not to miss the relevant studies. All key terms and concepts should be covered and checked to ensure that every study is present. All meta-analytic studies' functions are almost the same and follow a similar workflow. A research question should first be formulated to focus on an area of research. Then, the primary and secondary objectives must be defined. Identifying the relevant literature and constructing the search strategy are the next stages. The studies are screened and extracted based on the coding protocol, and the moderator variables are determined. Then, data analysis is completed to provide recommendations for future research. As seen in Fig. 3.1, the present study's design started by investigating and gathering the hypotheses generated in the primary studies. After rapid reviews, the hypotheses were regenerated and reappraised to find suggestions for future research.

3.4 Study Identification and Retrieval

The present analysis is limited to research published during the last 22 years in pragmatic instruction on the speech acts of request, apology, and refusal from 2000 to 2022. Electronic and manual searches were done to avoid missing any data and find all the full-text papers and dissertations on L2 pragmatic instruction. Many Applied Linguistics databases were used to search the relevant studies, including Springer Link, Web of Science, Microsoft Academic Search, Wiley Online Library, Research Gate, ScienceDirect, Google Scholar, Oxford Journals Digital Archive, iSEEK Education, Sage Journals Online, ProQuest, SAGE Knowledge, Magiran, Noormags, Project MUSE, ERIC, Blackwell Reference Online, RefSeek, Scopus, PhycINFO, Academic Index, Internet Public Library. Additionally, the keywords "meta-analysis", "pragmatics", "instruction", "speech acts", "request", "apology", and "refusal" were utilized to collect the data. Finally, the end references of related papers were checked to further reduce the possibility of missing studies. Interestingly, it was found that no meta-analysis had been conducted on the effectiveness of instruction of the speech acts of request, apology, and refusal.

3.5 Inclusion and Exclusion Criteria   33

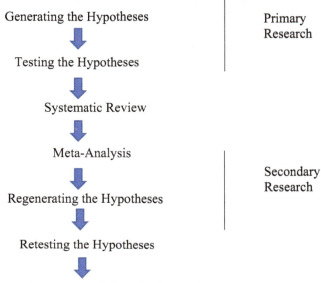

Fig. 3.1 Research design

3.5 Inclusion and Exclusion Criteria

To be included in this study, each empirical investigation had to meet the following criteria:

1. The studies had to be published between 2000 and 2022 (February) during the last 22 years, so papers earlier than 2000 or later than 2022 were excluded from the corpus.
2. The papers had to be published in English, so papers published in Persian, Chinese, Spanish, etc., were removed from the study.
3. The studies had to apply instruction on at least one of the speech acts of request, apology, or refusal; otherwise, they were not included in this study.
4. L2 pragmatic instruction was our focus in collecting the data, so L1 pragmatic papers were also excluded from the study.
5. The papers had to report sufficient data for calculating the effect sizes to be used in this study; in other words, papers in which means, standard deviations, and sample sizes were missing were also excluded.

After conducting the inclusion and exclusion criteria, 89 eligible sources out of 144 papers were found on the instruction of request, apology, and refusal, and 234 effect sizes based on the inclusion and exclusion criteria were included in this meta-analysis (Fig. 3.2).

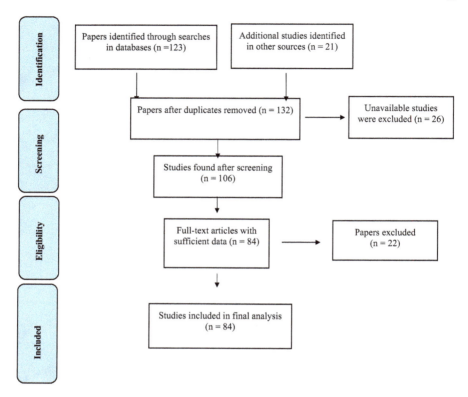

Fig. 3.2 Study retrieval process

3.6 Effect Size Calculation

To reach the total effect sizes utilized in this study, a standard mean difference (a weighted estimate of the difference between comparison and treatment groups) was applied (Borenstein, 2009). The effect sizes used in this study were calculated as Hedge's g, a measure to represent the standardized difference among means that is considered less biased than Cohen's d. Although these two statistics are almost the same, when the sample sizes are below 20, Hedge's g is preferable (Ellis, 2010). CMA (Version 3) was used to analyze the data, and the results are reported in the tables and figures in the next chapter.

3.7 Coding of Moderator Variables

The coding schema used in this study is based on the data gathered and categorized from the primary studies. Age, gender, proficiency level, research design, psycholinguistic features, treatment type, outcome measure, and the speech act type are among

3.7 Coding of Moderator Variables

the selected variables to be analyzed. Considering the age of the participants, participants 18 and under were coded as −18, and the next group of higher education students above 18 were categorized as +18 in the coding protocol. The studies in which the age was not reported were labeled as a not-reported group in the coding schema. Moreover, gender was coded as female, male, mixed, and not reported to be checked in the present study. The checked proficiency levels included elementary, intermediate, lower-intermediate, upper-intermediate, advanced, mixed, and not reported. Regarding the study's design, experimental and quasi-experimental studies were selected to be categorized in the present meta-analysis. Another coding section was devoted to the psycholinguistic features in which the comprehension and production of these three speech acts were used. The comprehension section included studies concerning the recognition and comprehension of the speech acts. Considering the production of speech acts, the studies that focused on pragmatic use were included in our corpus. There were also some studies using both comprehension and production, so a mixed group was defined for that category. Regarding treatment type, the studies were coded as explicit, implicit, both, and other teaching methods. Explicit studies were operationalized as studies in which a direct way of teaching was used to teach L2 pragmatics. Implicit ones were the studies through which the learners deduced the pragmatic knowledge on their own. Both included studies in which explicit and implicit were used together. Other teaching methods included other methods of teaching such as (a) deductive, (b) inductive, (c) Bloom-based, and (d) web-based instruction. The next moderator was the outcome measure coded as MDCT, WDCT, mixed (MDCT & WDCT), other, or not reported. The last section, speech act types, classified the speech acts as request, apology, refusal, and other speech acts called the mixed category since the primary purpose of this study was on the first three acts. The coding scheme (Table 3.1) was developed based on other experts' and peers' recommendations, suggestions in research on L2 pragmatics, and according to the previously conducted meta-analyses.

Table 3.1 Coding protocol

Features	Descriptors
Age	+18/−18/not reported
Gender	Female/male/mixed/not reported
Proficiency level	Elementary/intermediate/lower-intermediate/upper-intermediate/advanced/mixed/not reported
Design	Experimental/quasi-experimental
Psycholinguistic features	Comprehension/production/mixed
Treatment type	Explicit/implicit/both/other teaching methods
Outcome measure	MDCT, WDCT, mixed/other/not reported
Speech act type	Request, apology, refusal, mixed

3.8 Missing Data

In this meta-analysis, the landscape of the rapid development of L2 pragmatic instruction during the last decades on different speech acts, particularly request, apology, and refusal, was carried out by comparing and synthesizing previous empirical results and findings on instructional effectiveness. While searching for the key terms, 144 studies were found in which instruction is used in L2 pragmatics on the speech acts of request, apology, and refusal in various contexts worldwide. Among these studies, some focused on other pragmatic features such as implicatures, routines, and so on (Rafieyan, 2016; Rafieyan et al., 2014), so they were removed from the corpus of the study. Other studies lacked enough data to be added to the corpus (Alcón-Soler, 2012; Halenko & Jones, 2011; Shirazi et al., 2016; Takimoto, 2008, 2009; Teng & Fi, 2013) or were based on frequency-based analysis (Cunningham, 2016; Farrokhi & Atashian, 2013; Kim & Taguchi, 2015; Myrset, 2022; Nguyen, 2018), so they were also excluded. Moreover, several papers concerning comparison (Matsumura, 2022; Shark, 2019) were also eliminated from the corpus. Finally, studies using qualitative design (Ishihara, 2007; Kondo, 2004, 2008; Purwanti, 2018) were also excluded because only quantitative results can be used in meta-analyses. After the final screening, 84 studies met the coding criteria and were included in the present study for further analysis.

3.9 Reliability

The coding reliability was measured through the Rayyan website (www.rayyan.ai), a web and mobile application for systematic reviews and meta-analyses powered by artificial intelligence. This platform provides researchers with collaboration tools for blind rating and smart screening of papers. Following the data search and collection, all papers along with bibliographic information, were exported to Rayyan. Out of 144 primary studies, 84 studies were selected to be added to the present meta-analysis. After some sessions, the final decisions concerning inclusion and exclusion criteria were made and the coding schema became as transparent as possible, gaining a reliability index of 96%.

3.10 Publication Bias

Publication bias is a problem inherent in any method of study retrieval. It occurs because journals are much more likely to publish studies with more significant findings, which threatens meta-analyses. When checking the amount of publication bias, studies with larger sample sizes, small sampling errors, and high mean effect size values are located at the top of the graph (Plonsky & Gass, 2011). The remaining studies with small sample sizes and large sampling errors are placed on the right side of the mean. Two types of analyses can be carried out to identify publication bias: funnel plots and trim-and-fill analysis. First, funnel plots are a useful graphic tool to check if the treatment effects are influenced by publication bias. Funnel plots compare the effect sizes to standard errors, and if there is no bias, the plot shows a symmetrical inverted funnel. On the other hand, an unsymmetrical plot means some publication bias is present in the analysis. Second, is a trim-and-fill analysis that can address the issue of missing studies and publication bias.

References

Alcón-Soler, E. (2012). Teachability and bilingualism effects on third language learners' pragmatic knowledge. *Intercultural Pragmatics, 9,* 511–541. https://doi.org/10.1515/ip-2012-0028

Borenstein, M. (2009). Effect sizes for continuous data. In H. Cooper, L. V. Hedges, & J. C. Valentine (Eds.), *The handbook of research synthesis and meta-analysis* (pp. 221–235). Russell Sage Foundation.

Cunningham, D. J. (2016). Request modification in synchronous computer-mediated communication: The role of focused instruction. *The Modern Language Journal, 100*(2), 484–507.

DeLuca, J. B., Mullins, M. M., Lyles, C. M., Crepaz, N., Kay, L., & Thadiparthi, S. (2008). Developing a comprehensive search strategy for evidence based systematic reviews. *Evidence Based Library and Information Practice, 3*(1), 3–32.

Ellis, P. D. (2010). *The essential guide to effect sizes: Statistical power, meta-analysis, and the interpretation of research results.* Cambridge University Press.

Farrokhi, F., & Atashian, S. (2013). Towards pragmatic instruction of apology in Iranian context. *The Iranian EFL Journal, 1*(2), 207–241.

Glass, G. (1976). Primary, secondary, and meta-analysis of research. *Education Researcher, 5*(10), 3–8.

Halenko, N., & Jones, C. (2011). Teaching pragmatic awareness of spoken requests to Chinese EAP learners in the UK: Is explicit instruction effective? *System, 39*(2), 240–250.

Ishihara, N. (2007). Web-based curriculum for pragmatics instruction in Japanese as a foreign language: An explicit awareness-raising approach. *Language Awareness, 16*(1), 21–40.

Kim, Y., & Taguchi, N. (2015). Promoting task-based pragmatics instruction in EFL classroom contexts: The role of task complexity. *The Modern Language Journal, 99*(4), 656–677.

Kondo, S. (2004). Raising pragmatic awareness in the EFL context. *Sophia Junior College Faculty Bulletin, 24,* 49–72.

Kondo, S. (2008). Effects on pragmatic development through awareness-raising instruction: Refusals by Japanese EFL learners. *Investigating pragmatics in foreign language learning, teaching and testing,* 153–177.

Matsumura, S. (2022). The impact of predeparture instruction on pragmatic development during study abroad: A learning strategies perspective. *Study Abroad Research in Second Language Acquisition and International Education, 7*(1), 152–175.

Myrset, A. (2022). 'You could win Masterchef with this soup. Can I get some more?' Request production and the impact of instruction on young EFL learners. *Journal of Pragmatics, 192,* 56–76.

Nguyen, T. T. M. (2018). Pragmatic development in the instructed context: A longitudinal investigation of L2 email requests. *Pragmatics, 28*(2), 217–252.

Plonsky, L., & Gass, S. (2011). Quantitative research methods, study quality, and outcomes: The case of interaction research. *Language Learning, 61*(2), 325–366.

Plonsky, L., & Oswald, F. L. (2014). How big is "big"? Interpreting effect sizes in L2 research. *Language Learning, 64*(4), 878–912. https://doi.org/10.1111/lang.12079

Purwanti, I. T. (2018). *Pragmatic instruction effects on students' EFL production: A qualitative analysis*. Proceedings of the UR International Conference on Educational Sciences, Pekanbaru, Indonesia, 48–55.

Rafieyan, V. (2016). Effect of "focus on form" versus "focus on forms" pragmatic instruction on development of pragmatic comprehension and production. *Journal of Education and Practice, 7*(20), 41–48.

Rafieyan, V., Sharafi-Nejad, M., Khavari, Z., Eng, L. S., & Mohamed, A. R. (2014). Pragmatic comprehension development through telecollaboration. *English Language Teaching, 7*(2), 11–19.

Shakki, F. (2022). Meta-analysis as an emerging trend to scrutinize the effectiveness of L2 pragmatic instruction. *Frontiers in Psychology, 13*. https://doi.org/10.3389/fpsyg.2022.101666

Shakki, F., Naeini, J., Mazandarani, O., & Derakhshan, A. (2020). Instructed second language English pragmatics in the Iranian context. *Journal of Teaching Language Skills, 39*(1), 201–252. https://doi.org/10.22099/jtls.2020.38481.2886

Shark, P. (2019). The effects of explicit/implicit instructions on the development of advanced EFL learners' pragmatic knowledge of English: Apology speech act. *Journal of Language Teaching and Research, 10*(1), 76–82.

Shirazi, M., Ahmadi, S. D., & Mehrdad, A. G. (2016). The effect of using video games on EFL learners' acquisition of speech acts of apology and request. *Theory and Practice in Language Studies, 6*(5), 1019–1026.

Takimoto, M. (2008). The effects of deductive and inductive instruction on the development of language learners' pragmatic competence. *The Modern Language Journal, 92*(3), 369–386.

Takimoto, M. (2009). The effects of input-based tasks on the development of learners' pragmatic proficiency. *Applied Linguistics, 30*(1), 1–25.

Teng, C., & Fei, F. (2013). A consciousness-raising approach to pragmatics teaching: Web-based tasks for training study-abroad students. *Journal of Technology and Chinese Language Teaching, 4*(1), 50–63.

Chapter 4
Results

4.1 Introduction

Considering the inclusion and exclusion criteria we developed in the previous chapter, out of the 144 primary studies, 84 were selected to be analyzed in the present study. Among the primary studies, some papers did not have enough data, or they had descriptive or frequency-based analyses, so they were excluded from the analysis. In this chapter, the final selected corpus is analyzed to identify the effectiveness of pragmatic instruction and the variables that may moderate this effectiveness.

4.2 Description of the Included Corpus

The final sample used for further analysis consisted of 84 eligible studies with 234 effect sizes, and the description and details of the studies are presented in Table 4.1. Furthermore, the Frequency of the effect sizes obtained for each sub-component, namely speech act, outcome measure, treatment type, psycholinguistic features, age, gender, proficiency level, and design, is presented in Table 4.2.

4.2.1 Effect Size Frequency for the Speech Act Variable

Figure 4.1 shows the frequency of the effect sizes generated for each speech act included in the coding protocol. As can be seen, out of 84 studies with 234 effect sizes, 85 effect sizes were generated based on the speech act of request, 65 effect sizes for the mixed group in which a combination of the speech acts (request, apology, and refusal) was used, the speech act of apology yielded 46 effect sizes, and 38 effect sizes also were produced based on the speech act of refusal. Similar to what was

Table 4.1 Description of the included corpus

Study name	Measurement	Time point	Instruction	Psycholinguistic feature	Speech act	Age	Gender	Design	Proficiency
Anani Sarab & Alikhani (2016)	WDCT, MDCT	Posttest	Explicit	Production, Comprehension	Apology	Above 18	Female	Quasi	Advanced
Bagheri & Hamrang (2013)	WDCT, MDCT	Posttest	Explicit	Production, Comprehension	Apology	Above 18	Not mentioned	Experimental	Intermediate
Bagherkazemi (2018)	WDCT	Posttest	Other	Production	Apology	Above 18	Both	Quasi	Pre-intermediate
Eslami-Rasekh & Mardani (2010)	WDCT	Posttest	Explicit	Production	Apology	Above 18	Both	Experimental	Not Mentioned
Katchamat (2018)	WDCT	Posttest	Other	Production	Apology	Not Mentioned	Not Mentioned	Quasi	Pre-intermediate
Kargar, Sadighi & Ahmadi (2012)	WDCT, Other	Posttest, Delayed	Explicit, Implicit, Other	Production	Apology	Above 18	Both	Experimental	Pre-intermediate
Khodareza & Lotfi (2013)	WDCT, MDCT	Posttest	Explicit	Production, Comprehension	Apology	Not Mentioned	Not Mentioned	Quasi	Advanced
Pourmousavi & Mohamadi Zenouzagh (2020)	Other	Posttest	Other	Production	Apology	Above 18	Both	Quasi	Pre-intermediate
Rajabi, Azizifara & Gowhary (2015a)	WDCT	Posttest	Explicit	Production	Apology	Below 18	Female	Experimental	Intermediate

(continued)

4.2 Description of the Included Corpus

Table 4.1 (continued)

Study name	Measurement	Time point	Instruction	Psycholinguistic feature	Speech act	Age	Gender	Design	Proficiency
Rajabi, Azizifara & Gowhary (2015b)	WDCT	Posttest	Explicit	Production	Apology	Below 18	Female	Experimental	Intermediate
Razavi (2015)	WDCT	Posttest	Other	Production	Apology	Above 18	Not Mentioned	Experimental	Advanced
Sabzalipour & Koosha (2016)	MDCT	Posttest	Other	Comprehension	Apology	Not Mentioned	Not Mentioned	Experimental	Intermediate
Zangoei et al. (2014)	MDCT	Posttest	Other	Comprehension	Apology	Both	Both	Quasi	Upper-intermediate
Ahmadian (2020)	WDCT, MDCT	Posttest, Delayed	Explicit, Implicit	Production, Comprehension	Refusal	Above 18	Both	Experimental	Upper-intermediate
Soler & Pitarch (2010)	WDCT	Posttest	Explicit	Production	Refusal	Above 18	Both	Quasi	Not Mentioned
Bashang & Zenouzagh (2021)	WDCT	Posttest	Other	Production	Refusal	Below 18	Female	Quasi	Intermediate
Duong (2016)	WDCT	Posttest	Explicit	Production	Refusal	Above 18	Both	Experimental	Not Mentioned
Duong (2016)	WDCT	Posttest	Implicit	Production	Refusal	Above 18	Both	Experimental	Not Mentioned
Duong (2016)	WDCT	Delayed	Explicit	Production	Refusal	Above 18	Both	Experimental	Not Mentioned
Duong (2016)	WDCT	Delayed	Implicit	Production	Refusal	Above 18	Both	Experimental	Not Mentioned
Farahian, Rezaee & Gholami (2012)	WDCT	Posttest	Explicit	Production	Refusal	Above 18	Not Mentioned	Quasi	Intermediate

(continued)

41

Table 4.1 (continued)

Study name	Measurement	Time point	Instruction	Psycholinguistic feature	Speech act	Age	Gender	Design	Proficiency
Farahian, Rezaee & Gholami (2012)	WDCT	Delayed	Explicit	Production	Refusal	Above 18	Not Mentioned	Quasi	Intermediate
Gharibeh, Mirzaee & Yaghoubi-Notash (2016)	WDCT	Posttest	Explicit	Production	Refusal	Above 18	Both	Quasi	Upper-intermediate
Haghighi et al. (2019)	WDCT	Posttest	Other	Production	Refusal	Above 18	Both	Experimental	Intermediate
Halenko & Flores-Salgado (2020)	WDCT	Posttest	Other	Production	Refusal	Above 18	Both	Experimental	Pre-intermediate
Hernández (2021)	Other	Posttest	Explicit	Production	Refusal	Above 18	Both	Experimental	Not Mentioned
Hamuoody & Jasim (2011)	WDCT	Posttest	Explicit	Mixed	Refusal	Not Mentioned	Both	Experimental	Not Mentioned
Nipaspong & Chinokul (2008)	Other	Posttest	Other	Production	Refusal	Above 18	Not Mentioned	Quasi	Mixed
Nipaspong & Chinokul (2010)	MDCT	Posttest	Other	Comprehension	Refusal	Both	Both	Quasi	Mixed
Shirinbakhsh et al. (2018)	Other	Posttest, Delayed	Explicit, Other	Production	Refusal	Above 18	Female	Quasi	Mixed
Soler and Pitarch (2010)	Other	Posttest	Explicit	Production	Refusal	Above 18	Both	Quasi	Not Mentioned
Abdullahizadeh Masouleh et al. (2014)	MDCT	Posttest	Explicit	Comprehension	Request	Above 18	Female	Experimental	Intermediate

(continued)

4.2 Description of the Included Corpus   43

Table 4.1 (continued)

Study name	Measurement	Time point	Instruction	Psycholinguistic feature	Speech act	Age	Gender	Design	Proficiency
Ahmadi et al. (2011)	WDCT, MDCT	Posttest, Delayed	Other	Production, Comprehension	Request	Above 18	Both	Experimental	Mixed
Alcón-Soler (2015a)	WDCT	Posttest, Delayed, Post Delayed	Explicit	Production	Request	Both	Not mentioned	Quasi	Upper-intermediate
Alcón-Soler (2015b)	WDCT	Posttest, Delayed, Post Delayed	Explicit	Production	Request	Above 18	Both	Quasi	Upper-intermediate
Alcón-Soler (2017)	WDCT	Posttest	Explicit	Production	Request	Below 18	Not mentioned	Experimental	Intermediate
Anami Sarab & Alikhani (2016)	WDCT, MDCT	Posttest	Explicit	Comprehension	Request	Above 18	Female	Quasi	Advanced
Barekat & Mehri (2013)	WDCT	Posttest	Other	Production	Request	Both	Male	Quasi	Intermediate
Canbolat et al. (2021)	MDCT	Posttest	Explicit	Comprehension	Request	Below 18	Not mentioned	Quasi	Not mentioned
Eslami, Mirzaei & Dini (2015)	WDCT	Posttest	Explicit, Implicit	Production	Request	Above 18	Both	Experimental	Upper-intermediate
Fakher Ajabshir (2018)	WDCT	Posttest	Explicit	Production	Request	Above 18	Both	Experimental	Pre-intermediate
Fakher Ajabshir (2022)	WDCT, Other	Posttest	Other	Production, Comprehension	Request	Above 18	Female	Experimental	Intermediate

(continued)

Table 4.1 (continued)

Study name	Measurement	Time point	Instruction	Psycholinguistic feature	Speech act	Age	Gender	Design	Proficiency
Fathi & Feozollahi (2023)	WDCT	Posttest	Explicit, Implicit	Production	Request	Above 18	Both	Experimental	Intermediate
Hernández & Boero (2018)	WDCT	Posttest	Explicit	Production	Request	Above 18	Both	Quasi	Not Mentioned
Kaivanpanah & Langari (2020)	WDCT	Posttest, Delayed	Other	Production	Request	Below 18	Not Mentioned	Quasi	Not Mentioned
Malaz et al. (2011)	WDCT	Posttest	Other	Production	Request	Not Mentioned	Female	Quasi	Intermediate
Omanee and Krishnasamy (2019)	WDCT	Posttest	Other	Production	Request	Above 18	Both	Experimental	Pre-intermediate
Rajabi, Azizifar & Gowhary (2015b)	WDCT	Posttest	Explicit	Production	Request	Below 18	Female	Experimental	Intermediate
Rezvani, Eslami-Rasekh & Vahid Dastjerdi (2014)	WDCT	Posttest	Explicit, Implicit	Production	Request	Above 18	Not Mentioned	Experimental	Intermediate
Saadatmandi et al. (2018)	MDCT	Posttest	Explicit	Comprehension	Request	Below 18	Female	Experimental	Pre-intermediate
Sadeqi & Ghaemi (2016)	WDCT, MDCT	Posttest	Explicit	Production, Comprehension	Request	Above 18	Both	Quasi	Advanced
Taguchi & Kim (2016)	WDCT	Posttest, Delayed	Explicit	Production	Request	Below 18	Female	Experimental	Pre-intermediate

(continued)

4.2 Description of the Included Corpus

Table 4.1 (continued)

Study name	Measurement	Time point	Instruction	Psycholinguistic feature	Speech act	Age	Gender	Design	Proficiency
Tajjedin & Hosseinpur (2014a)	WDCT	Posttest	Other	Production	Request	Above 18	Both	Quasi	Not Mentioned
Tajjedin & Hosseinpur (2014b)	WDCT	Posttest, Delayed, Post Delayed	Other	Production	Request	Above 18	Both	Experimental	Upper-intermediate
Usó-Juan (2022)	Other	Posttest	Other	Production	Request	Above 18	Both	Quasi	Upper-intermediate
Xiao-Le (2011)	WDCT	Posttest	Explicit, Implicit	Production	Request	Above 18	Not Mentioned	Experimental	Advanced
Ziashahabi et al. (2020)	MDCT	Posttest, Delayed	Explicit, Implicit	Comprehension	Request	Both	Female	Experimental	Intermediate
Bagherkazemi & Harati-Asl (2022)	WDCT	Posttest	Other	Production	Mixed	Above 18	Male	Quasi	Intermediate
Bayındır (2019)	WDCT	Posttest	Explicit	Production	Mixed	Above 18	Both	Experimental	Advanced
Bataineh et al. (2017)	WDCT	Posttest	Other	Production	Mixed	Not mentioned	Not mentioned	Quasi	Not Mentioned
Birjandi and Derakhshan (2014)	MDCT	Posttest	Other	Comprehension	Mixed	Both	Both	Experimental	Upper-intermediate
Birjandi and Derakhshan (2014)	WDCT	Posttest	Other	Production	Mixed	Above 18	Not mentioned	Quasi	Not mentioned

(continued)

Table 4.1 (continued)

Study name	Measurement	Time point	Instruction	Psycholinguistic feature	Speech act	Age	Gender	Design	Proficiency
Boufira et al. (2022)	MDCT, WDCT, Mixed	Posttest	Other	Production, Comprehension, Mixed	Mixed	Not Mentioned	Not Mentioned	Quasi	Not Mentioned
Davarzani & Talebzadeh (2020)	MDCT	Posttest	Other	Comprehension	Mixed	Below 18	Female	Experimental	Intermediate
Derakhshan and Eslami (2015)	MDCT	Posttest	Other	Comprehension	Mixed	Both	Both	Experimental	Upper-intermediate
Derakhshan & Shakki (2020)	MDCT	Posttest	Explicit	Comprehension	Mixed	Above 18	Both	Experimental	Intermediate
Djouani & Hadjeris (2017)	MDCT	Posttest	Explicit	Comprehension	Mixed	Above 18	Not Mentioned	Quasi	Not Mentioned
Eslami-Rasekh, Eslami-Rasekh, & Fatahi (2004)	WDCT	Posttest	Explicit	Comprehension	Mixed	Above 18	Both	Experimental	Advanced
Fakher & Panahifar (2020)	WDCT	Posttest	Other	Production	Mixed	Above 18	Both	Experimental	Intermediate
Iraji et al. (2018)	MDCT	Posttest	Explicit	Comprehension	Mixed	Both	Both	Experimental	Upper-intermediate
Khatib & Ahmadi Safa (2011)	WDCT, MDCT	Posttest	Explicit, Implicit, Mixed	Production, Comprehension	Mixed	Not Mentioned	Both	Experimental	Mixed
Mirzaee & Esmaeili (2013)	WDCT, MDCT	Posttest	Explicit	Production, Comprehension	Mixed	Above 18	Both	Quasi	Not Mentioned
Mouna (2016)	Mixed	Posttest	Explicit	Mixed	Mixed	Not Mentioned	Not Mentioned	Experimental	Not Mentioned

(continued)

4.2 Description of the Included Corpus

Table 4.1 (continued)

Study name	Measurement	Time point	Instruction	Psycholinguistic feature	Speech act	Age	Gender	Design	Proficiency
Nemati & Arabmofrad (2014)	WDCT, MDCT	Posttest	Other	Production, Comprehension	Mixed	Not Mentioned	Not Mentioned	Experimental	Not Mentioned
Nguyen et al. (2012)	WDCT, Other	Posttest	Explicit, Implicit	Production	Mixed	Not Mentioned	Both	Quasi	Not Mentioned
Salehi (2011)	WDCT	Posttest	Implicit	Production	Mixed	Above 18	Both	Quasi	Not Mentioned
Tajeddin & Bagherkazemi (2014)	WDCT	Posttest, Delayed	Other	Production	Mixed	Above 18	Both	Quasi	Intermediate
Tajeddin et al. (2012)	WDCT	Posttest	Other	Production	Mixed	Above 18	Both	Experimental	Intermediate
Tanaka & Oki (2015)	Other	Posttest	Explicit	Comprehension	Mixed	Above 18	Not Mentioned	Quasi	Not Mentioned
Zand-Moghadam & Samani (2021)	WDCT	Posttest	Other	Production	Mixed	Both	Both	Experimental	Intermediate
Ziafar (2020)	MDCT	Posttest	Implicit, Explicit, Other	Comprehension	Mixed	Not Mentioned	Both	Experimental	Not Mentioned
Omanee (2021)	WDCT	Posttest	Other	Production	Apology, Request	Above 18	Both	Experimental	Pre-intermediate
Gaily (2014)	WDCT	Posttest	Other	Production	Apology, Request, Refusal, Other	Above 18	Male	Quasi	Not Mentioned

(continued)

Table 4.1 (continued)

Study name	Measurement	Time point	Instruction	Psycholinguistic feature	Speech act	Age	Gender	Design	Proficiency
Halenko & Flores-Salgado (2020)	WDCT	Posttest	Other	Production	Other	Above 18	Both	Experimental	Pre-intermediate

4.2 Description of the Included Corpus

Table 4.2 Frequency of the extracted effect sizes for each sub-component

		Frequency	Percent	Valid percent	Cumulative percent
Speech Act	Apology	46	19.2	19.2	19.2
	Refusal	38	16.2	16.2	35.4
	Request	85	35.9	35.9	71.3
	Mixed	65	27.8	27.8	99.1
	Total	234	100.0	100.0	
Outcome Measure	MDCT	51	21.8	21.8	21.8
	WDCT	142	60.7	60.7	82.5
	Mixed	2	0.9	0.9	83.4
	Other	39	16.6	16.6	100.0
	Total	234	100.0	100.0	
Treatment Type	Explicit	103	44.0	44.0	44.0
	Implicit	26	11.1	11.1	55.1
	Mixed	2	0.9	0.9	56.0
	Other	103	44.0	44.0	100.0
	Total	234	100.0	100.0	
Psycholinguistic Feature	Comprehension	56	23.9	23.9	23.9
	Production	172	73.5	73.5	97.4
	Mixed	6	2.6	2.6	100.0
	Total	234	100.0	100.0	
Age	Above 18	129	55.1	55.1	55.1
	Below 18	35	15.0	15.0	70.1
	Both	25	10.7	10.7	80.8
	Not Mentioned	45	19.2	19.2	100.0
	Total	234	100.0	100.0	
Gender	Male	8	3.4	3.4	3.4
	Female	61	26.1	26.1	29.5
	Both	124	53.0	53.0	82.5
	Not Mentioned	41	17.5	17.5	100.0
	Total	234	100.0	100.0	
Proficiency Level	Pre-intermediate	56	23.9	23.9	23.9
	Intermediate	57	24.4	24.4	48.3
	Upper-intermediate	29	12.4	12.4	60.7
	Advanced	16	6.8	6.8	69.5
	Mixed	22	9.4	9.4	78.9
	Not Mentioned	54	23.1	23.1	100.0

(continued)

Table 4.2 (continued)

		Frequency	Percent	Valid percent	Cumulative percent
	Total	234	100.0	100.0	
Design	Quasi	83	35.5	35.5	100.0
	Experimental	151	64.5	64.5	64.5
	Total	234	100.0	100.0	

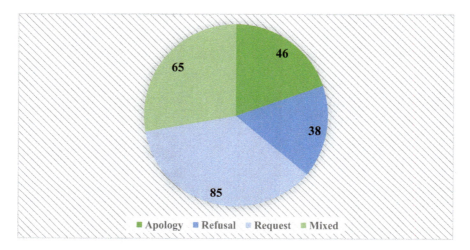

Fig. 4.1 Effect size frequency for the speech acts

found by Shakki et al. (2020) in the Iranian context, the speech act of request was considered the most dominant speech act used in the research conducted during the last two decades worldwide, followed by apology and refusal.

4.2.2 Effect Size Frequency for the Outcome Measure Variable

MDCTs and WDCTs are common outcome measures used for various types of data collection in pragmatic research (Shakki et al., 2020). Figure 4.2 gives information about the frequency of the effect sizes generated based on the coding protocol. Overall, we see that out of 234 effect sizes, 142 effects were produced on WDCTs, 51 effects for MDCTs, 2 effects for the mixed group, and 39 effects for other outcome measures. The notable increase in WDCTs use in this study is not in line with Shakki et al. (2020) results, where MDCTs were the most frequent outcome measures, but

4.2 Description of the Included Corpus   51

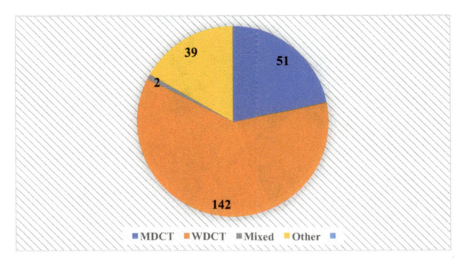

Fig. 4.2 Effect size frequency for the outcome measures

these findings are consistent with Shakki et al. (2023) in which WDTCs with 47 effects were used more than MDCTs.

4.2.3 Effect Size Frequency for Treatment Type Variable

Reviewing the papers published between 2000 to 2022 revealed that different treatment types were used to instruct pragmatics during these decades. Regarding the coding protocol criteria, the explicit group generated 103 effects, the implicit group 26, the mixed group in which both explicit and implicit interventions are used generated 2 effects, and other treatment types such as input enhancement, metapragmatic awareness, deductive and inductive teaching produced 103 effects (Fig. 4.3). Similar results were found after comparing these frequencies with the only study with the same criteria in an Iranian context (Shakki et al., 2020). They reported that out of 79 effect sizes, 25 were yielded on the explicit vs. implicit and control groups, while 24 effects were on the explicit vs. control group. The last 30 effects belonged to other treatment types such as dictogloss, consciousness-raising, form search, interactive translation, discussion, role play, etc.

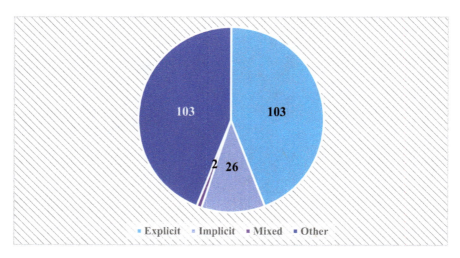

Fig. 4.3 Effect size frequency for the treatment types

4.2.4 Effect Size Frequency for the Psycholinguistic Feature Variable

Interestingly, out of 234 effects, 172 effect sizes were yielded for production, whereas 56 effects focus on comprehension. Figure 4.4 clearly represents the superiority of pragmatic production over pragmatic comprehension in our view. Six effects were produced for the mixture of both comprehension and production. On the contrary, studies in Iran reported by Shakki et al. (2023) showed more tendency for comprehension (42 effects) than production (37 effects).

4.2.5 Effect Size Frequency for the Age Variable

Taking Fig. 4.5 into account, the participants aged 18 and above generated 129 effects, while those under 18 produced 35 effects. The group of both above and below 18 generated 25 effects, and the not mentioned group (the age of the participants was not reported) yielded 45 effect sizes. Similar to Shakki et al.'s (2023) study, the above 18 participants were the most dominant learners selected in the research during the last 22 years. This shows that higher education students are being studied by most researchers worldwide.

4.2 Description of the Included Corpus

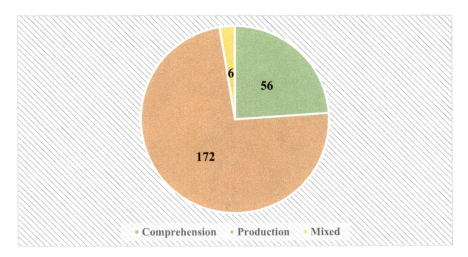

Fig. 4.4 Effect size frequency for the psycholinguistic features

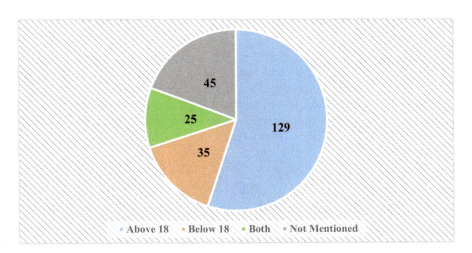

Fig. 4.5 Effect size frequency for the age

4.2.6 *Effect Size Frequency for the Gender Variable*

As seen in Fig. 4.6, the most frequent group is the one in which both genders (male and female) participated. One hundred twenty-nine effects were generated for both genders, 61 for females, 41 for males, and 8 effects were produced from the not-mentioned studies. The frequency of the effect sizes demonstrated that most researchers prefer to use both genders in their studies, and if they were supposed to focus on one specific gender, females received special attention.

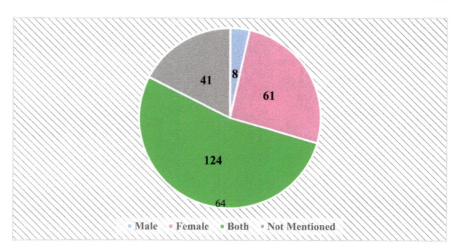

Fig. 4.6 Effect size frequency for gender

4.2.7 *Effect Size Frequency for the Proficiency Level Variable*

Proficiency level, another vital factor in each study, was covered and reported in the following order: pre-intermediate level generated 56 effects; intermediate level, 57; upper-intermediate, 29; advanced learners, 16; mixed students, 22; and the not-mentioned group, 54. Figure 4.7 illustrates that there is no significant difference between intermediate and pre-intermediate learners, and they have been the dominant proficiency levels studied during the last decades.

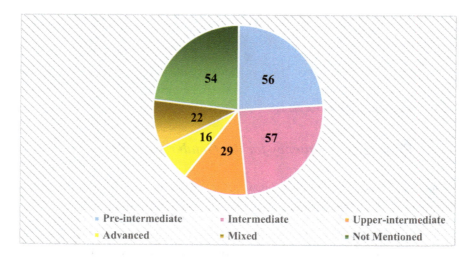

Fig. 4.7 Effect size frequency for proficiency levels

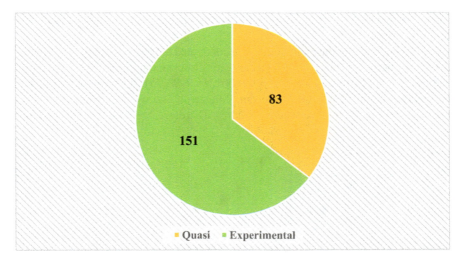

Fig. 4.8 Effect size frequency for study designs

4.2.8 *Effect Size Frequency for the Design Variable*

The design of the conducted studies was defined as experimental or quasi-experimental, and there was a significant difference between these two groups (Fig. 4.8). The experimental design generated 151, while the quasi-experimental produced 83 effect sizes, which means that most studies have been conducted with an experimental design.

4.3 Overall Effectiveness of L2 Pragmatic Instruction

The 234 effect sizes extracted then were explored to answer the first research question of the study, the overall effectiveness of L2 pragmatic instruction for the speech acts of request, apology, and refusal. In this section, the main results will first be presented; then, the results will be tested for publication bias.

4.3.1 *Main Results*

Figure 4.9 shows the plot of the estimations. Statistical analysis of the results (see Appendix) showed that all effect sizes were significant except for a few studies at 95% confidence intervals. The effect sizes vary greatly from −0.201 to 7.551. Table 4.3 presents the analysis's main results, including the average weighted Hedges' *g*, the 95% prediction intervals, the Q-test for heterogeneity, the two-tailed test of null, and the percentage of variation between studies due to heterogeneity rather than sampling error.

Before interpreting the main results, we conducted the heterogeneity test. The test of heterogeneity was significant, demonstrating substantial variability between the studies ($Q = 3726.156$, $df = 233$, $p < 0.001$, $I^2 = 93.75$). It also indicates that all the variance is unlikely to be due to sampling error, and we also conclude that the true effect size is likely to vary across studies. Therefore, we used the random effect

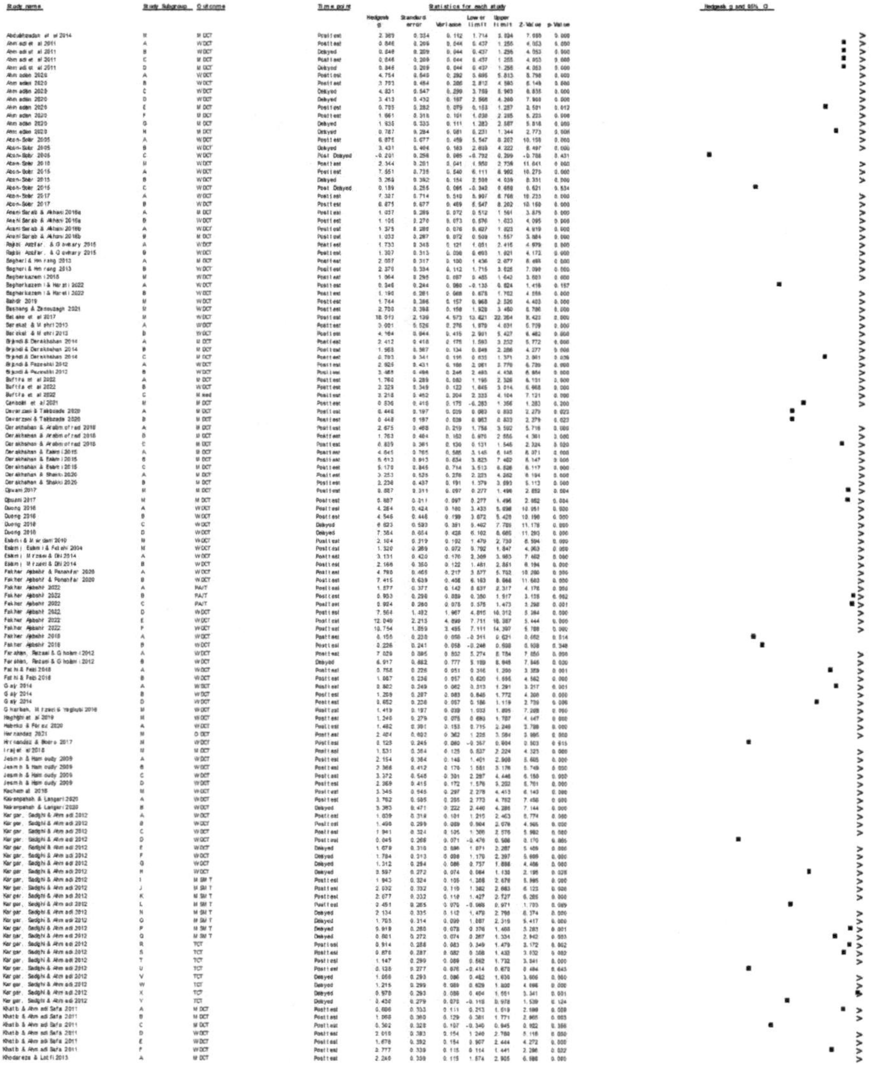

Fig. 4.9 High-resolution forest plot of the effect sizes for all included studies

4.3 Overall Effectiveness of L2 Pragmatic Instruction

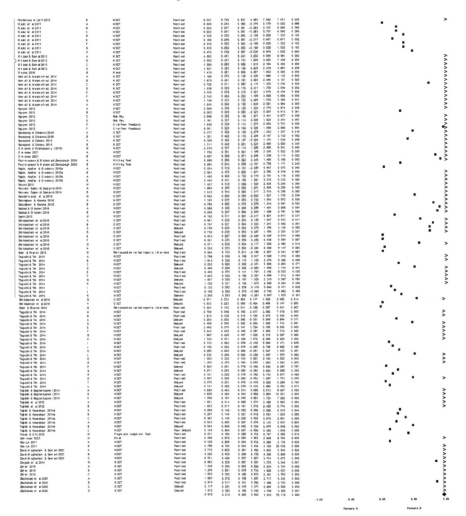

Fig. 4.9 (continued)

model, as it is the best fit when the data shows significant heterogeneity (Borenstein et al., 2011). The tau-square value was 1.111, which shows a very large correlation among the effect sizes. The overall effect size (random effect) was found to be 1.720, with a standard error of 0.073, a z-value for a test of the null of 23.472, and a corresponding p-value of less than 0.001. Based on Plonsky and Oswald (2014), the field-specific benchmarks for effect size interpretation for L2 researchers, this average effect size was considered large.

Table 4.3 Main results of meta-analysis for the overall effect of L2 pragmatic instruction

	N	g	SE	95% CI	Test of null Z	P	Heterogeneity Q	df	p	I^2	Tau-Squared τ^2	se	τ
Fixed effect	234	0.982	0.018	[0.947, 1.017]	55.520	0.000	3729.156	233	0.000	93.75	1.111	0.038	1.050
Random effect	234	1.720	0.073	[1.576, 1.864]	23.472	0.000							

Note N = number of effect sizes, g = mean weighted effect size in Hedges' *g*, SE = standard error, CI = confidence interval, Z = Z value, P = P value, Q = Cochran's heterogeneity test; df = degrees of freedom, τ^2 = between-study variance; I^2 = percentage of variation between studies that is due to heterogeneity rather than sampling error

4.3.2 Publication Bias

In order to avoid or decrease publication bias in meta-analyses, we used a number of different procedures. First, the Trim and Fill method (Duval & Tweedie, 2000) was utilized to assess publication bias (Table 4.4). This method uses a procedure to eliminate the most extreme small studies from the positive side of the funnel plot, iteratively re-computing the effect size until the funnel plot is symmetric (Borenstein et al., 2009). Under the fixed-effect model, the combined studies' point estimate and 95% confidence interval is 0.977. Using Trim and Fill, the value changed to 0.583 (0.552, 0.615). Under the random-effects model, the combined studies' point estimate and 95% confidence interval is 1.662. Using Trim and Fill, the value changed to 0.679 (0.522, 0.835); therefore, it can be concluded that all studies' effect sizes are medium after adjustment.

The results reported in Table 4.4 indicate that 93 extreme values on the positive side should be compensated for. In other words, these results are affected by publication bias. Figure 4.10 depicts the funnel plot for observed (circles in white) and imputed values (circles in black).

Second, Orwin's (1983) fail-safe N was inspected. The test estimates the number of missing studies (with a mean effect of zero) that would need to be added to

Table 4.4 Duval and Tweedie's trim and fill test of publication bias estimation

	Studies trimmed	Fixed effects		Random effects		Q value
		Point estimate	(Lower, upper)	Point estimate	(Lower, upper)	
Observed values		0.97963	(0.9452, 1.0140)	1.6617	(1.5221, 1.8012)	3599.8545
Adjusted values	93	0.58333	(0.5517, 0.6150)	0.6785	(0.5222, 0.8348)	7622.7132

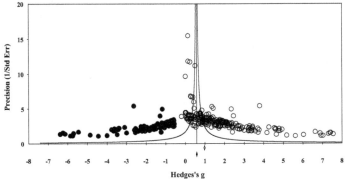

Fig. 4.10 Funnel plot of precision by effect sizes for the observed and imputed studies

the analysis to yield a statistically non-significant overall effect. The result (Nfs = 293,467) was high, indicating that synthesized values of effect sizes were reliable and publication bias was negligible.

4.4 Overall Effectiveness of L2 Pragmatic Instruction on the Speech Act of Apology

To show a detailed result of the effectiveness of instruction on the improvement of the speech acts, the three frequent speech acts used in the corpus were separately analyzed. The first speech act was apology.

4.4.1 Main Results for the Effectiveness of Instruction Focused on Apology

Overall, 45 effect sizes were obtained from the speech act of apology studies. Figure 4.11 shows the high-resolution plot of the estimations.

An inspection of the results showed that, except for four, all effect sizes were significant at 95% confidence intervals. The effect sizes vary moderately from 0.045 to 6.027. Table 4.5 presents the analysis's main results, including the average weighted Hedges'g, the 95% prediction intervals, the Q-test for heterogeneity, the two-tailed test of null, and the percentage of variation between studies due to heterogeneity rather than sampling error.

Before interpreting the main results, we conducted the heterogeneity test. The test of heterogeneity was significant, demonstrating substantial variability between the studies ($Q = 250.316$, $df = 44$, $p < 0.001$, $I^2 = 82.422$). It also indicates that all the variance is unlikely to be due to sampling error, and we also conclude that the true effect size is likely to vary across studies. Therefore, we used the random effect model (Borenstein et al., 2011). The tau-square value turned out to be 0.422, which shows a medium correlation among the effect sizes. The overall effect size (random effect) for the speech act of apology was 1.394, with a standard error of 0.108, a z-value for a test of the null of 12.935, and a corresponding p-value of less than 0.001. Based on Plonsky and Oswald (2014), the field-specific benchmarks for effect size interpretation for L2 researchers, this average effect size was considered large.

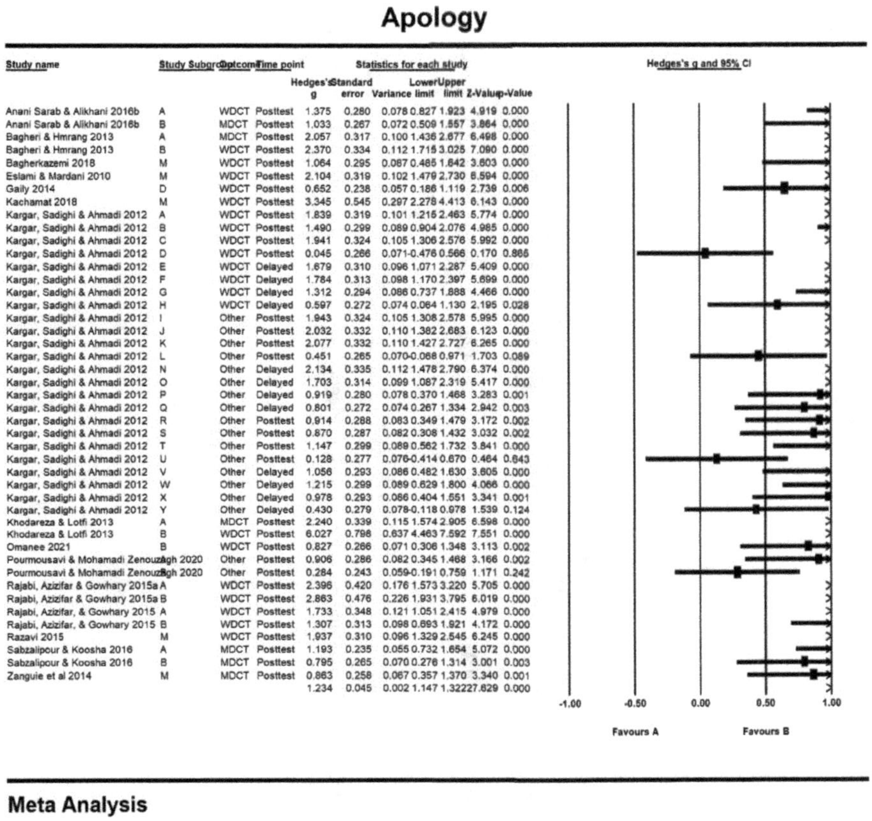

Apology

Fig. 4.11 Forest plot of the effect sizes for the speech act of apology

4.4.2 Publication Bias

In order to avoid or decrease publication bias in the meta-analyses, we used a number of different procedures. First, Trim and Fill, a method developed by Duval and Tweedie (2000), was utilized to assess publication bias (Table 4.6). The method uses a procedure to eliminate the most extreme small studies from the positive side of the funnel plot, iteratively re-computing the effect size until the funnel plot is symmetric (Borenstein et al., 2009). Under the fixed-effect model, the combined studies' point estimate and 95% confidence interval is 1.234. Using Trim and Fill, the value changed to 1.066 (0.926, 1.087). Under the random-effects model, the combined studies' point estimate and 95% confidence interval is 1.393. Using Trim and Fill, the value changed to 0.1.04 (0.808, 1.272). Therefore, it can be concluded that the effect size for the speech act of apology slightly changed after the adjustment and remained large.

Table 4.5 Main results of meta-analysis for the speech act of apology

					Test of null		Heterogeneity			Tau-squared			
	N	g	SE	95% CI	Z	P	Q	df	p	I^2	τ^2	se	τ
Fixed effect	45	1.234	0.045	[1.147, 1.342]	27.629	0.000	250.316	44	0.000	82.422	0.422	0.112	0.649
Random effect	45	1.394	0.108	[1.183, 1.605]	12.935	0.000							

Note N = number of effect sizes, g = mean weighted effect size in Hedges' g, SE = standard error, CI = confidence interval, Z = Z value, P = P value, Q = Cochran's heterogeneity test; df = degrees of freedom, τ^2 = between-study variance; I^2 = percentage of variation between studies that is due to heterogeneity rather than sampling error

4.4 Overall Effectiveness of L2 Pragmatic Instruction on the Speech Act ...

Table 4.6 Duval and Tweedie's trim and fill test of publication bias estimation: Speech act of apology

	Studies trimmed	Fixed effects		Random effects		Q value
		Point estimate	(Lower, upper)	Point estimate	(Lower, upper)	
Observed values		1.23409	(1.1466, 1.3216)	1.39286	(1.1827, 1.6051)	250.3158
Adjusted values	12	1.0066	(0.9259, 1.0873)	1.03992	(0.8076, 1.2722)	452.7741

The results reported in Table 4.6 indicate that 12 extreme values on the positive side should be compensated for. In other words, the results are affected by publication bias. Figure 4.12 depicts the funnel plot for observed (circles in white) and imputed values (circles in black).

Second, Orwin's (1983) fail-safe N was inspected. The test estimates the number of missing studies (with a mean effect of zero) that would need to be added to the analysis to yield a statistically non-significant overall effect. The result (Nfs = 10,103) was high, indicating that synthesized values of effect sizes were reliable and publication bias was negligible.

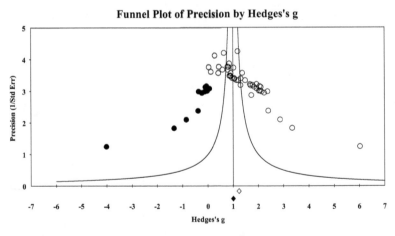

Fig. 4.12 Funnel plot of precision by effect sizes for the observed and imputed studies: Speech act of apology

4.5 Overall Effectiveness of L2 Pragmatic Instruction on the Speech Act of Refusal

The next speech act to be examined was refusal. The results obtained from the corpus of the study for this speech act are presented below.

4.5.1 Main Results for the Effectiveness of Instruction Focused on Refusals

Overall, 38 effect sizes were obtained from the studies. Figure 4.13 shows the high-resolution plot of the estimations.

The inspection of the results showed that, except for a few studies, all effect sizes were significant at 95% confidence intervals. The effect sizes vary moderately from 0.001 to 7.384. Table 4.7 presents the analysis's main results, including the average weighted Hedge's g, the 95% prediction intervals, the Q-test for heterogeneity, the two-tailed test of null, and the percentage of variation between studies due to heterogeneity rather than sampling error.

Before interpreting the main results, we conducted the heterogeneity test. The heterogeneity test was significant, demonstrating substantial variability between the studies ($Q = 462.466$, $df = 37$, $p < 0.001$, $I^2 = 95.71$). It also indicated that all

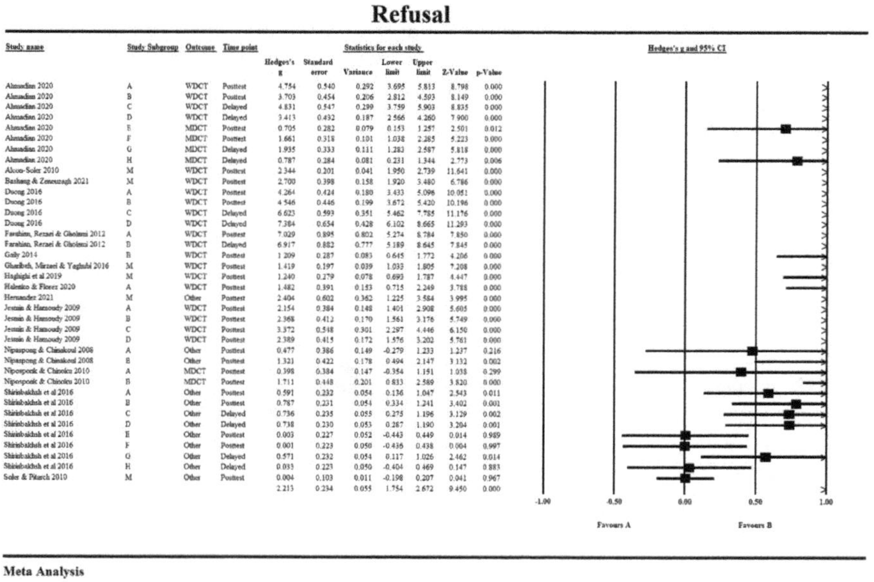

Fig. 4.13 Forest plot of the effect sizes for the speech act of refusal

4.5 Overall Effectiveness of L2 Pragmatic Instruction on the Speech Act …

Table 4.7 Main results of meta-analysis for the speech act of refusal

	N	g	SE	95% CI	Test of null Z	P	Heterogeneity Q	df	p	I^2	Tau-squared τ^2	se	τ
Fixed effect	38	1.126	0.047	[1.035, 1.217]	24.196	0.000	462.466	37	0.000	95.710	1.915	0.679	1.384
Random effect	38	2.213	0.234	[1.754, 2.672]	9.450	0.000							

Note N = number of effect sizes, g = mean weighted effect size in Hedges' g, SE = standard error, CI = confidence interval, Z = Z value, P = P value, Q = Cochran's heterogeneity test; df = degrees of freedom, τ^2 = between-study variance; I^2 = percentage of variation between studies that is due to heterogeneity rather than sampling error

the variance is unlikely to be due to sampling error, and we also conclude that the true effect size is likely to vary across studies. Therefore, we used the random effect model (Borenstein et al., 2011). The tau-square value was 1.915, showing a strong correlation among the effect sizes. The overall effect size (random effect) for the refusal speech act was 2.213, with a standard error of 0.234, a z-value for a test of the null of 9.45, and a corresponding p-value of less than 0.001. Based on Plonsky and Oswald (2014), the field-specific benchmarks for effect size interpretation for L2 researchers, this average effect size was considered very large.

4.5.2 Publication Bias

In order to avoid or decrease publication bias in meta-analyses, we used a number of different procedures. First, the Trim and Fill method (Duval & Tweedie, 2000) was used to assess publication bias (Table 4.8). The method uses a procedure to eliminate the most extreme small studies from the positive side of the funnel plot, iteratively re-computing the effect size until the funnel plot is symmetric (Borenstein et al., 2009). Under the fixed-effect model, the combined studies' point estimate and 95% confidence interval is 1.126. Using Trim and Fill, the value changed to 0.716 (0.630, 0.802). Under the random-effects model, the combined studies' point estimate and 95% confidence interval is 2.213. Using Trim and Fill, the value changed to 0.828 (0.325, 1.331). Therefore, it can be concluded that the effect size for the speech act of refusal significantly changed after adjustment to medium.

The results reported in Table 4.8 indicate that 15 extreme values on the positive side should be compensated for. In other words, the results are affected by the publication bias. Figure 4.14 depicts the funnel plot for observed (circles in white) and imputed values (circles in black).

Second, Orwin's (1983) fail-safe N was inspected. The test estimates the number of missing studies (with a mean effect of zero) that would need to be added to the analysis to yield a statistically non-significant overall effect. The result (Nfs = 10,160) was high, indicating that synthesized values of effect sizes were reliable and publication bias was negligible.

Table 4.8 Duval and Tweedie's trim and fill test of publication bias estimation: Speech act of refusal

	Studies trimmed	Fixed effects		Random effects		Q value
		Point estimate	(Lower, upper)	Point estimate	(Lower, upper)	
Observed values		1.1257	(1.0345, 1.2169)	2.2129	(1.7539, 2.6719)	862.4659
Adjusted values	15	0.7161	(0.6302, 0.8019)	0.8284	(0.3255, 1.3314)	1669.4477

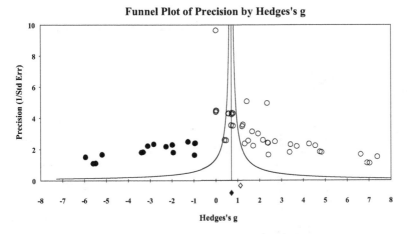

Fig. 4.14 Funnel plot of precision by effect sizes for the observed and imputed studies: Speech act of refusal

4.6 Overall Effectiveness of L2 Pragmatic Instruction on the Speech Act of Request

The speech act of request was the following speech act for which the standardized effectiveness was calculated. The results of the analyses are provided below.

4.6.1 Main Results of the Effectiveness of Instruction Focused on Request

Overall, 84 effect sizes were obtained from the studies. Figure 4.15 shows the high-resolution plot of the estimations.

The inspection of the results showed that, except for a handful of studies, all effect sizes were significant at 95% confidence intervals. The effect sizes vary moderately from −0.201 to 7.551. Table 4.9, below, presents the analysis's main results, including the average weighted Hedges' g, the 95% prediction intervals, the Q-test for heterogeneity, the two-tailed test of null, and the percentage of variation between studies due to heterogeneity rather than sampling error.

Before interpreting the main results, we conducted the heterogeneity test. The heterogeneity test was significant, demonstrating a substantial variability between the studies ($Q = 1476.19$, $df = 83$, $p < 0.001$, $I^2 = 94.377$). It also indicated that all the variance is unlikely to be due to sampling error, and we also conclude that the true effect size is likely to vary across studies. Therefore, we used the random effect model (Borenstein et al., 2011). The tau-square value was 0.874, showing a strong correlation among the effect sizes. The overall effect size (random effect) for the

Request

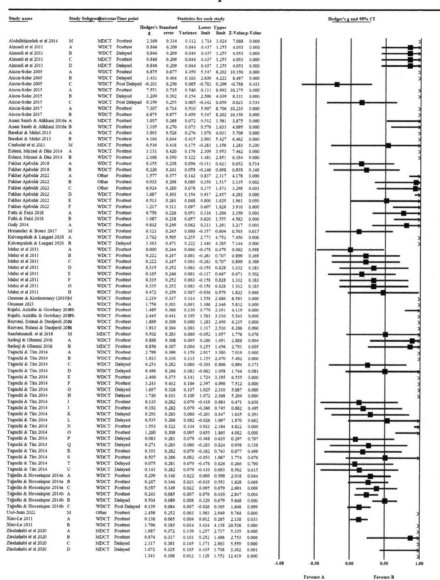

Meta Analysis

Fig. 4.15 Forest plot of the effect sizes for the speech act of request

4.6 Overall Effectiveness of L2 Pragmatic Instruction on the Speech Act …

Table 4.9 Main results of meta-analysis for the speech act of request

	N	g	SE	95% CI	Test of null Z	Test of null P	Heterogeneity Q	Heterogeneity df	Heterogeneity p	I^2	Tau-squared τ^2	Tau-squared se	τ
Fixed effect	84	0.692	0.024	[0.644, 0.740]	28.310	0.000	1476.190	83	0.000	94.377	0.874	0.262	0.935
Random effect	38	1.341	0.108	[1.129, 1.552]	12.419	0.000							

Note N = number of effect sizes, g = mean weighted effect size in Hedges' g, SE = standard error, CI = confidence interval, Z = Z value, P = P value, Q = Cochran's heterogeneity test; df = degrees of freedom, τ^2 = between-study variance; I^2 = percentage of variation between studies that is due to heterogeneity rather than sampling error

speech act of request was 1.341, with a standard error of 0.108, a z-value for a test of the null of 12.419, and a corresponding p-value of less than 0.001. Based on Plonsky and Oswald (2014), the field-specific benchmarks for effect size interpretation for L2 researchers, this average effect size was considered large.

4.6.2 Publication Bias

In order to avoid or decrease publication bias in meta-analyses, we used a number of different procedures. First, Trim and Fill, a method developed by Duval and Tweedie (2000), was utilized to assess publication bias (Table 4.10). The method uses a procedure to eliminate the most extreme small studies from the positive side of the funnel plot, iteratively re-computing the effect size until the funnel plot is symmetric (Borenstein et al., 2009). Under the fixed-effect model, the combined studies' point estimate and 95% confidence interval is 0.692. Using Trim and Fill, the value changed to 0.384 (0.339, 0.429). Under the random-effects model, the combined studies' point estimate and 95% confidence interval is 1.341. Using Trim and Fill, the value changed to 0.453 (0.208, 0.698). Therefore, it can be concluded that the effect size for the speech act of request changed after adjustment to medium.

The results reported in Table 4.10 indicate that 30 extreme values on the positive side should be compensated for. In other words, the results are affected by the publication bias. Figure 4.16 depicts the funnel plot for observed (circles in white) and imputed values (circles in black).

Second, Orwin's (1983) fail-safe N was inspected. The test estimates the number of missing studies (with a mean effect of zero) that would need to be added to the analysis to yield a statistically non-significant overall effect. The result (Nfs = 29,590) was high, indicating that synthesized values of effect sizes were reliable and publication bias was negligible.

Table 4.10 Duval and Tweedie's trim and fill test of publication bias estimation: Speech act of request

	Studies trimmed	Fixed effects		Random effects		Q value
		Point estimate	(Lower, upper)	Point estimate	(Lower, upper)	
Observed values		0.6923	(0.6443, 0.7402)	1.3407	(1.1291, 1.5523)	1476.1895
Adjusted values	30	0.3838	(0.3388, 0.4289)	0.4530	(0.2084, 0.6979)	3119.1560

4.7 Moderating Effects of L2 Pragmatic Instruction

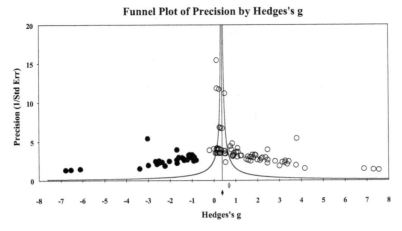

Fig. 4.16 Funnel plot of precision by effect sizes for the observed and imputed studies: Speech act of request

4.7 Moderating Effects of L2 Pragmatic Instruction

The moderating effects of seven variables were examined on the effect size to answer the second research question on the variables that moderate the effectiveness of L2 pragmatic instruction, especially the speech acts of request, apology, and refusal. These variables were either demographic features of the participants (age, gender, language proficiency) or design-related factors (design of the study, measurement tool, psycholinguist feature measured, type of treatment, and type of speech act). The results are presented in the following sub-sections.

4.7.1 Demographic Features

The demographic features as the moderating factor of the effectiveness of instruction on improving speech acts were investigated.

4.7.1.1 Age

Q-tests were used to evaluate if the particular variable was a significant moderator of the instruction of pragmatics for the speech acts of request, apology, and refusal. Table 4.11 shows the results of moderator analysis for the participant's ages.

As seen in Table 4.11, the moderator analysis results for the participants' age ($Q = 8.752$, $df = 3$, $p = 0.033$) displayed a significant moderating effect on the results. Pairwise comparisons were made to locate the place of significant differences.

Table 4.11 Mixed effects moderator analysis: Age of the participants

Categories	N	g	S.E	95%CI	Q^b	df	p
Above 18	129	1.667	0.095	[1.480, 1.854]			
Below 18	35	1.583	0.204	[1.183, 1.983]			
Mixed	25	2.450	0.293	[1.877, 3.023]			
Not Mentioned	45	1.501	0.139	[1.229, 1.773]			
Overall	234	1.660	0.071	[1.117, 1.374]			
Total Between					8.752	3	0.033

Note N = total number of participants, g = mean weighted effect size in Hedges' *g*, CI = confidence interval, P = P-value, Q^b = Q-between, df = degrees of freedom

Table 4.12 Pairwise comparison of effect sizes: Age of the participants

A	B	Q^b	p
Above 18	Below 18	0.139	0.709
	Mixed	6.474	0.011
	Not Mentioned	0.973	0.324
Below 18	Mixed	5.907	0.015
	Not Mentioned	0.110	0.740
Mixed	Not Mentioned	8.589	0.003

As reported in Table 4.12, studies with mixed age groups reported significantly higher effect sizes than the other three categories.

4.7.1.2 Gender

Another demographic feature considered as a variable for the effectiveness of L2 pragmatic instruction was the participant's gender. Table 4.13 demonstrates the results of the mixed effects moderator analysis.

As is evident from Table 4.13, the number of effect sizes obtained from male participants was limited. Therefore, the analysis was conducted once for the total studies and once after the exclusion of male participants. Both analyses showed significant results, indicating that the gender of the participants was a significant moderator. Pairwise comparisons were then conducted to determine the differences (Table 4.14).

The results in Table 4.14 show that the studies that did not report the gender of the participants had significantly higher effect sizes than the other three groups. Moreover, studies that included both genders had significantly higher effect sizes than those that only included females. While the limited number of male participants makes the results for this group less reliable, from the content of the studies, it could be inferred that most of the studies that did not specify the gender of the participants tended to use both genders. Therefore, it is safe to conclude that the

4.7 Moderating Effects of L2 Pragmatic Instruction

Table 4.13 Mixed effects moderator analysis: Gender of the participants

Categories	N	g	S.E	95%CI	Q^b	df	p
Male	8	1.380	0.289	[0.814, 1.946]			
Female	61	0.977	0.095	[0.790, 1.163]			
Both	124	1.830	0.101	[1.633, 2.028]			
Not Mentioned	41	2.538	0.248	[2.052, 3.024]			
Overall	234	1.459	0.065	[1.331, 1.586]			
Total Between					58.257	3	0.000
Males Excluded					58.178	2	0.000

Note N = total number of participants, g = mean weighted effect size in Hedges' *g*, CI = confidence interval, P = P-value, Q^b = Q-between, df = degrees of freedom

Table 4.14 Pairwise comparison of effect sizes: Gender of the participants

A	B	Q^b	p
Male	Female	1.754	0.185
	Both	2.170	0.141
	Not Mentioned	9.264	0.002
Female	Both	37.922	0.000
	Not Mentioned	34.539	0.000
Both	Not Mentioned	6.996	0.008

heterogeneity of the participants in terms of gender works as a significant moderator in the effectiveness of speech act instructions.

4.7.1.3 Proficiency Level

The final demographic feature to be examined as a moderator was the participants' level of language proficiency. The results of the Q-tests are reported in Table 4.15.

As reported in Table 4.15, proficiency level was also a significant moderator ($Q = 58.26, p = 0.000$). Two categories of "advanced" and "mixed" had a limited number of extracted effect sizes. The exclusion of these two also kept the results significant. Pairwise comparisons were run to compare the results between the groups (Table 4.16).

The results reported in Table 4.16 indicate that the studies that included participants with mixed levels of language proficiency extracted significantly lower effect sizes than all other categories. The pre-intermediate level also had significantly lower effect sizes than all other language proficiency levels except for the studies with mixed levels. No significant difference was found between participants with intermediate, upper-intermediate, and advanced levels, and the treatment seemed to work

Table 4.15 Mixed effects moderator analysis: Participants' proficiency level

Categories	N	g	S.E	95%CI	Q^b	df	p
Pre-intermediate	56	1.082	0.101	[0.883, 1.280]			
Intermediate	57	2.024	0.166	[1.698, 2.349]			
Upper-intermediate	29	2.404	0.238	[1.940, 2.872]			
Advanced	16	1.815	0.352	[1.126, 2.505]			
Mixed	22	0.733	0.098	[0.542, 0.924]			
Not Mentioned	54	1.922	0.164	[1.600, 2.245]			
Overall	234	1.274	0.058	[1.161, 1.387]			
Total Between					58.257	5	0.000
Advanced Excluded					92.902	4	0.000
Mixed Excluded					77.606	4	0.000

Note N = total number of participants, g = mean weighted effect size in Hedges' g, CI = confidence interval, P = P-value, Q^b = Q-between, df = degrees of freedom

Table 4.16 Pairwise comparison of effect sizes: Participants' proficiency level

A	B	Q^b	p
Pre-intermediate	Intermediate	23.47	0.000
	Upper-intermediate	26.267	0.000
	Advanced	4.014	0.045
	Mixed	6.153	0.013
	Not Mentioned	18.957	0.000
Intermediate	Upper-intermediate	1.740	0.187
	Advanced	0.287	0.592
	Mixed	44.920	0.000
	Not Mentioned	0.188	0.665
Upper-intermediate	Advanced	1.938	0.164
	Mixed	42.375	0.000
	Not Mentioned	2.801	0.094
Advanced	Mixed	8.786	0.003
	Not Mentioned	0.076	0.782
Mixed	Not Mentioned	38.694	0.000

significantly better with these groups. The studies that did not mention the participants' level of proficiency also showed similar results to those with intermediate, upper-intermediate, and advanced participant levels.

4.7 Moderating Effects of L2 Pragmatic Instruction

Table 4.17 Mixed effects moderator analysis: Design of the studies

Age	N	g	S.E	95%CI	Q^b	df	p
Experimental	151	1.718	0.008	[1.545, 1.892]			
Quasi	83	1.562	0.015	[1.325, 1.799]			
Overall	234	1.664	0.071	[1.523, 1.804]			
Total Between					1.092	1	0.296

Note N = total number of participants, g = mean weighted effect size in Hedges' g, CI = confidence interval, P = P-value, Q^b = Q-between, df = degrees of freedom

4.7.2 Design-Related Features

The next series of moderators were categorized under the design-related variables. These moderators concerned the design of the study, the outcome measure, the psycholinguist features, the type of treatments, and the type of speech acts.

4.7.2.1 Design

Q-tests were used to evaluate if the particular variable was a significant moderator. Table 4.17 shows the results of the moderating effect of the studies' design.

As seen in Table 4.17, the results of moderator analysis for the design of the studies ($Q = 1.092, df = 1, p = 0.296$) showed no significant difference between the two types of design. Therefore, this feature is not considered a predictive moderator for the effectiveness of L2 pragmatic instruction for the mentioned speech acts.

4.7.2.2 Outcome Measure

The next moderator variable to be examined was the measurement tools used to measure the outcome of the studies. The overall results are reported in Table 4.18.

As reported in Table 4.18, the number of studies using mixed measurement tools was too limited (N = 2). Hence, the results obtained from this category were not precise, as indicated by the large standard error (SE) and the broad interval confidence. Therefore, these two studies were removed from the moderator analysis. After removing these studies, the results of the Q-test ($Q = 34.69, df = 2, p = 0.000$) were still significant, indicating that the variable works as a moderator. Pairwise comparisons were made to locate where the differences lie (Table 4.19).

As the results in Table 4.19 indicate, the effect sizes obtained from WDCT were significantly higher than those obtained from both MDCT and other tools. Moreover, the effect sizes obtained from MDCT were significantly higher than those obtained from other tools.

Table 4.18 Mixed effects moderator analysis: Outcome measure

Categories	N	g	S.E	95%CI	Q^b	df	p
MDCT	51	1.475	0.112	[1.255, 1.696]			
WDCT	142	1.911	0.103	[1.710, 2.712]			
Mixed	2	2.276	0.904	[0.505, 4.047]			
Other	39	1.004	0.115	[1.710, 2.112]			
Overall	234	1.502	0.063	[1.379, 1.626]			
Total Between					35.405	3	0.000
Mixed Excluded					34.668	2	0.000

Note N = total number of participants, g = mean weighted effect size in Hedges' *g*, CI = confidence interval, P = P-value, Q^b = Q-between, df = degrees of freedom

Table 4.19 Pairwise comparison of effect sizes: Outcome measure

A	B	Q^b	p
MDCT	WDCT	8.191	0.004
	Other	8.608	0.003
WDCT	Other	34.606	0.000

4.7.2.3 Psycholinguistic Feature

The psycholinguistic feature was another moderating variable. It should be noted that this factor was closely related to the study's measurement tools, as the studies tended to use MDCT to measure comprehension and WDCT to evaluate production. Table 4.20 shows the overall results of this variable.

As reported in Table 4.20, the number of extracted effect sizes for mixed psycholinguistic features was too limited ($N = 6$). The large SE and wide confidence intervals also acknowledged that the data obtained from this category might not be reliable. However, after excluding this category, the comparison between comprehension and

Table 4.20 Mixed effects moderator analysis: Psycholinguistic feature

Categories	N	g	S.E	95%CI	Q^b	df	p
Comprehension	56	1.425	0.103	[1.223, 1.628]			
Production	172	1.704	0.087	[1.534, 1.875]			
Mixed	6	2.414	0.317	[1.792, 3.036]			
Overall	234	1.624	0.065	[1.496, 1.751]			
Total Between					10.737	2	0.005
Mixed Excluded					4.260	1	0.039

Note N = total number of participants, g = mean weighted effect size in Hedges' *g*, CI = confidence interval, P = P-value, Q^b = Q-between, df = degrees of freedom

4.7 Moderating Effects of L2 Pragmatic Instruction

Table 4.21 Mixed effects moderator analysis: Treatment type

Categories	N	g	S.E	95%CI	Q^b	df	p
Explicit	103	1.890	0.126	[1.643, 2.137]			
Implicit	26	1.464	0.217	[1.038, 1.890]			
Mixed	2	0.532	0.237	[0.067, 0.997]			
Other	103	1.511	0.091	[1.332, 1.690]			
Overall	234	1.536	0.067	[1.404, 1.667]			
Total Between					25.976	3	0.000
Mixed Excluded					6.547	2	0.038

Note N = total number of participants, g = mean weighted effect size in Hedges' *g*, CI = confidence interval, P = P-value, Q^b = Q-between, df = degrees of freedom

Table 4.22 Pairwise comparison of effect sizes: Treatment type

A	B	Q^b	p
Explicit	Implicit	2.881	0.090
	Other	5.948	0.015
Implicit	Other	0.040	0.841

production was shown to be significant ($Q = 4.26$, $p = 0.039$), indicating that the effect sizes obtained from production were higher.

4.7.2.4 Treatment Type

The next moderating variable was the type of treatment. Table 4.21 shows the overall results for this variable.

The results in Table 4.21 show a limited number of effect sizes ($N = 2$) obtained from a mixed type of treatment. Such limited numbers cannot be relied upon. After excluding this category, the difference among the other types of treatments was significant ($Q = 6.55$, $df = 2$, $p = 0.038$), indicating that the type of treatment is a significant moderator. Pairwise comparisons (Table 4.22) were run to locate the differences.

The results in Table 4.22 indicate that the difference between explicit instruction of speech acts and other types of instructions was significant. No significant differences were found between explicit and implicit instruction and between implicit and other types of instruction.

4.7.2.5 Speech Act Type

The final moderating variable in the design-related features was the type of speech act. We have already presented the results for the three main types: apology, refusal, and request in Sects. 4.4, 4.5, and 4.6. The Q-test was run on the results to see if the variable serves as moderating variable (Table 4.23).

As reported in Table 4.23, the effect sizes obtained from other types of speech acts were limited in number (N = 2). After removing these effect sizes, the comparison results ($Q = 23.942$, $df = 3$, $p = 0.000$) among the remaining four categories were significant, indicating that the type of speech act is a significant moderator. Pairwise comparisons in Table 4.24 show the place of differences.

The results in Table 4.24 show that studies including refusal instruction rendered significantly larger effect sizes than those with apology and request. Moreover, studies with mixed speech acts in their designs had significantly higher effect sizes than apology and request speech acts. The difference between the effect sizes obtained for apology and request and for refusal and mixed speech acts were not statistically significant.

Table 4.23 Mixed effects moderator analysis: Speech act type

Categories	N	g	S.E	95%CI	Q^b	df	p
Apology	45	1.394	0.012	[1.183, 1.605]			
Refusal	38	2.213	0.234	[1.038, 1.890]			
Request	84	1.341	0.108	[1.129, 1.552]			
Mixed	65	1.993	0.139	[1.720, 2.266]			
Other	2	0.800	0.207	[0.394, 1.206]			
Overall	234	1.497	0.061	[1.377, 1.618]			
Total Between					36.372	4	0.000
Other Excluded					23.942	3	0.000

Note N = total number of participants, g = mean weighted effect size in Hedges' g, CI = confidence interval, P = P-value, Q^b = Q-between, df = degrees of freedom

Table 4.24 Pairwise comparison of effect sizes: Speech act type

A	B	Q^b	p
Apology	Refusal	10.096	0.001
	Request	0.121	0.728
	Mixed	11.579	0.001
Refusal	Request	11.441	0.001
	Mixed	0.652	0.419
Request	Mixed	13.705	0.000

References

Abdullahizadeh Masouleh, F., Arjmandi, M., & Vahdany, F. (2014). The effect of explicit metapragmatic instruction on request speech act awareness of intermediate EFL students at institute level. *Universal Journal of Educational Research, 2*(7), 504–511.

Ahmadi, A., Ghafar, S. R., & Yazdanimoghaddam, M. (2011). Teaching requestive downgraders in L2: How effective are input-based and output-based tasks? *Iranian Journal of Applied Linguistics (IJAL), 14*(2), 1–30.

Ahmadian, M. J. (2020). Explicit and implicit instruction of refusal strategies: Does working memory capacity play a role? *Language Teaching Research, 24*(2), 163–188.

Ajabshir, Z. F. (2018). The effect of synchronous and asynchronous computer-mediated communication (CMC) on EFL learners' pragmatic competence. *Computers in Human Behavior, 92*, 169–177.

Alcón-Soler, E. (2015a). Pragmatic learning and study abroad: Effects of instruction and length of stay. *System, 48*, 62–74.

Alcón-Soler, E. (2015b). Instruction and pragmatic change during study abroad email communication. *Innovation in Language Learning and Teaching, 9*(1), 34–45.

Alcón-Soler, E. (2017). Pragmatic development during study abroad: An analysis of Spanish teenagers' request strategies in English emails. *Annual Review of Applied Linguistics, 37*, 77–92.

Anani Sarab, M. R., & Alikhani, S. (2016). The efficacy of pragmatic instruction in EFL Context: The case of persian learners of English. *English Teaching & Learning, 40*(1), 25–48.

Bagheri, M., & Hamrang, A. (2013). The effect of meta pragmatic instructions on the interpretation and use of apology speech acts of English as a Foreign Language Learner (EFL) at intermediate level. *International Journal of Social Sciences & Education, 3*(4), 964–975.

Bagherkazemi, M. (2018). Impact of collaborative output-based instruction on EFL learners' awareness of the speech act of apology. *Journal of Language and Translation, 8*(4), 45–54.

Bagherkazemi, M., & Harati-Asl, M. (2022). Interlanguage pragmatic development: Comparative impacts of cognitive and interpersonal tasks. *Iranian Journal of Language Teaching Research, 10*(2), 37–54.

Barekat, B., & Mehri, M. (2013). Investigating the effect of metalinguistic feedback in L2 pragmatic instruction. *International Journal of Linguistics, 5*(2), 197–208.

Bashang, S., & Zenouzagh, Z. M. (2021). The effect of learner-centered instruction on Iranian EFL learners' critical thinking and pragmatic competence. *International Journal of Humanities and Social Science, 8*(5), 36–42.

Bataineh, R. F., Al-Qeyam, F. R., & Smadi, O. M. (2017). Does form-focused instruction really make a difference? Potential effectiveness in Jordanian EFL learners' linguistic and pragmatic knowledge acquisition. *Asian-Pacific Journal of Second and Foreign Language Education, 2*(1), 1–11.

Bayındır, S. (2019). *The effects of explicit teaching of speech acts on EFL learners' pragmatic competence* (Unpublished Master's thesis) İstanbul Sabahattin Zaim Üniversitesi, Sosyal Bilimler Enstitüsü, İngiliz Dili Eğitimi Anabilim Dalı.

Birjandi, P., & Derakhshan, A. (2014). The impact of consciousness-raising video-driven vignettes on the pragmatic development of apology, request, & refusal. *Applied Research on English Language, 3*(1), 67–85.

Borenstein, M. (2009). Effect sizes for continuous data. In H. Cooper, L. V. Hedges & J. C. Valentine (Eds.), *The handbook of research synthesis and meta-analysis* (pp. 221–235). Russell Sage Foundation.

Borenstein, M., Hedges, L. V., Higgins, J. P., & Rothstein, H. R. (2011). *Introduction to meta-analysis*. John Wiley & Sons, Ltd.

Bouftira, M., El Messaoudi, M., & Li, S. (2022). Developing EFL learners' pragmatic competence through a blended learning model: A quasi-experimental study. *European Scientific Journal, 18*(16), 105–132.

Canbolat, H. C., Atasoy, S., & Naiboglu, B. (2021). The effects of explicit pragmatic teaching on young learners' pragmatic development. *The Journal of International Lingual Social and Educational Sciences, 7*(1), 1–16.

Davarzani, F., & Talebzadeh, H. (2020). The effect of virtual and real classroom instruction on interlanguage pragmatic development: microblogging versus traditional instruction of speech acts to Iranian EFL learners. *Journal of English Language Pedagogy and Practice, 13*(27), 72–99.

Derakhshan, A., & Eslami, Z. R. (2015). The effect of consciousness-raising instruction on the comprehension of apology & request. *TESL-EJ, 18*(4). http://www.tesl-ej.org/wordpress/issues/volume18/ej72/ej72a6/

Derakhshan, A., & Shakki, F. (2020). The effect of implicit vs. explicit metapragmatic instruction on the Iranian intermediate EFL learners' pragmatic comprehension of apology and refusal. *Journal of Language Research, 12*(35), 151–175.

Djouani, S., & Hadjeris, F. (2017). *The effect of the explicit instruction of refusal strategies in fostering EFL learners' pragmatic competence* (Unpublished MA Thesis). Larbi Ben M'hidi University.

Duong, A. C. (2016). *Profiling the learning of pragmatic competencies in tertiary EFL classrooms in Vietnam: Critical reflections on the current debate around the efficacy of instructional pedagogies* (Unpublished Doctoral thesis). University of Newcastle, Australia.

Duval, S., & Tweedie, R. (2000). Trim and fill: A simple funnel-plot–based method of testing and adjusting for publication bias in meta-analysis. *Biometrics, 56*(2), 455–463.

Eslami, Z. R., Mirzaei, A., & Dini, S. (2015). The role of asynchronous computer mediated communication in the instruction and development of EFL learners' pragmatic competence. *System, 48*, 99–111. https://doi.org/10.1016/j.system.2014.09.008

Eslami-Rasekh, Z., Eslami-Rasekh, A., & Fatahi, A. (2004). The effect of explicit metapragmatic instruction on the speech act awareness of advanced EFL students. *TESL-EJ, 8*(2). http://cwp60.berkeley.edu:16080/TESL-EJ/ej30/a2.htm

Eslami-Rasekh, A., & Mardani, M. (2010). Investigating the effects of teaching apology speech act, with a focus on intensifying strategies, on pragmatic development of EFL learners: The Iranian context. *The International Journal of Language Society and Culture, 30*(1), 96–103.

Fakher Ajabshir, Z. (2022). The relative efficacy of input enhancement, input flooding, and output-based instructional approaches in the acquisition of L2 request modifiers. *Language Teaching Research, 26*(3), 411–433.

Fakher, Z., & Panahifar, F. (2020). The effect of teachers' scaffolding and peers' collaborative dialogue on speech act production in symmetrical and asymmetrical groups. *Iranian Journal of Language Teaching Research, 8*(1), 45–61.

Farahian, M., Rezaee, M., & Gholami, A. (2012). Does direct instruction develop pragmatic competence? Teaching refusals to EFL learners of English. *Journal of Language Teaching and Research, 3*(4), 814–821.

Fathi, J., & Feozollahi, B. (2023). The effects of deductive and inductive interventions on developing Iranian EFL learners' pragmatic competence: An investigation of the speech act of request. *Linguistic Studies: Theory and Practice, 1*(1), 163–176.

Gaily, M. M. A. (2014). Developing pragmatic competence of the Sudanese university EFL learners via planned classroom instruction. *International Journal of Social Science Arts Human, 1*, 40–49.

Gharibeh, S. G., Mirzaee, M., & Yaghoubi-Notash, M. (2016). The role of instruction in the development of EFL learners' pragmatic competence. *The Asian Journal of Applied Linguistics, 3*(2), 173–184.

Haghighi, H., Jafarigohar, M., Khoshsima, H., & Vahdany, F. (2019). Impact of flipped classroom on EFL learners' appropriate use of refusal: Achievement, participation, perception. *Computer Assisted Language Learning, 32*(3), 261–293.

Halenko, N., & Flores-Salgado, E. (2020). *Embedding ICT to teach and assess the pragmatic targets of refusals and disagreements in spoken English*. British Council ELT research papers.

Hernández, T. A. (2021). Explicit instruction for the development of L2 Spanish pragmatic ability during study abroad. *System, 96*, 102395.

References

Hernández, T. A., & Boero, P. (2018). Explicit intervention for Spanish pragmatic development during short-term study abroad: An examination of learner request production and cognition. *Foreign Language Annals, 51*(2), 389–410.

Hamuoody, B. A., & Jasim, B. Y. (2011). The impact of explicit instruction on developing pragmatic competence: A focus on refusal to offers. *Journal of Tikrit University for Humanities, 18*(7).

Iraji, H. R., Enayat, M. J., & Momeni, M. (2018). The effects of implicit and explicit instruction on the academic interlanguage pragmatic knowledge of Iranian EFL learners. *Language & Translation, 6*(1), 171–178.

Kaivanpanah, S., & Langari, M. T. (2020). The effect of Bloom-based activities and Vygotskian scaffolding on Iranian EFL learners' use of the speech act of request. *Current Psychology*. https://doi.org/10.1007/s12144-020-01053-z

Kargar, A. A., Sadighi, F., & Ahmadi, A. R. (2012). The effects of collaborative translation task on the apology speech act production of Iranian EFL learners. *The Journal of Teaching Language Skills, 4*(3), 47–78.

Katchamat, P. (2018). The effect of flipped classroom instruction on appropriacy of English apology by Thai EFL learners. *International Journal of Pedagogy and Teacher Education, 2*, 13–119.

Khatib, M., & Ahmadi Safa, M. (2001). The effectiveness of ZPD-wise explicit/implicit expert peers and coequals' scaffolding in ILP development. *Iranian Journal of Applied Linguistics, 14*, 49–75.

Khodareza, M., & Lotfi, A. R. (2013). Interlanguage pragmatic development: The effect of formal instruction on Iranian EFL learners' interpretation and use of speech act of apology. *Asian Journal of Social Sciences and Humanities, 2*(2), 99–104.

Malaz, I., Rabiee, M., & Ketabi, S. (2011). The pragmatic instruction effects on Persian EFL learners' noticing and learning outcomes in request forms. *Journal of Technology & Education, 5*(3), 187–193.

Mirzaee, A., & Esmaeili, M. (2013). The effects of planned instruction on Iranian L2 learners' interlanguage pragmatic development. International *Journal of Society, Culture & Language, 1*(1), 89–100.

Mouna, F. E. R. A. T. H. A. (2016). The effect of pragmatic instruction on the speech act awareness of third-year graduate students of English. *Mars*, 111.

Nemati, M., & Arabmofrad, A. (2014). Development of interlanguage pragmatic competence: input- and output-based instruction in the zone of proximal development. *Theory and Practice in Language Studies, 4*(2), 262–270.

Nguyen, T. T. M., Pham, T. H., & Pham, M. T. (2012). The relative effects of explicit and implicit form-focused instruction on the development of L2 pragmatic competence. *Journal of pragmatics, 44*(4), 416–434.

Nipaspong, P., & Chinokul, S. (2008). The effects of corrective feedback techniques on EFL learners' pragmatic production and confidence. *PASAA, 42*, 55–77.

Nipaspong, P., & Chinokul, S. (2010). The role of prompts and explicit feedback in raising EFL learners' pragmatic awareness. *University of Sydney Papers in TESOL, 5*(5), 101–146.

Omanee, B. (2021). *A pragmatic analysis of the effects of youtube in acquiring request and apology speech acts on Thai EFL hospitality undergraduates* (Unpublished Doctoral Dissertation). Universiti Utara Malaysia.

Omanee, B., & Krishnasamy, H. N. (2019). Pragmatic development of Thai EFL hospitality undergraduates through YouTube intervention instruction: A case of the speech act of request at hotel front desk service. *Journal of Applied Linguistics and Language Research, 6*(5), 79–94.

Orwin, R. G. (1983). A Fail-SafeN for effect size in meta-analysis. *Journal of Educational Statistics, 8*(2), 157–159. https://doi.org/10.3102/10769986008002157

Plonsky, L., & Oswald, F. L. (2014). How big is "big"? Interpreting effect sizes in l2 research. *Language Learning, 64*(4), 878–912. https://doi.org/10.1111/lang.12079

Pourmousavi, Z., & Zenouzagh, Z. M. (2020). A comparative study of the effect of teacher's group and individual feedback on Iranian EFL learners' learning of speech acts in apology letter writing. *Asian-Pacific Journal of Second and Foreign Language Education, 5*(1), 1–24.

Rajabi, S., Azizifara, A., & Gowhary, H. (2015a). The effect of explicit instruction on pragmatic competence development; Teaching requests to EFL learners of English. *Procedia-Social and Behavioral Sciences, 199*(3), 231–239.

Rajabi, S., Azizifara, A., & Gowhary, H. (2015b). Investigating the of explicit instruction of apology speech act on pragmatic development of Iranian EFL learners. *Advances in Language and Literary Studies, 6*(4), 53–61.

Razavi, A. (2015). Dynamic assessment and its impact on the acquisition of speech act of apology among Iranian advanced learners. *Proceedings of National Conference on Language, Literature and Translation in Education, Islamic Azad University, Meybod*, 1–7.

Rezvani, E., Eslami-Rasekh, A., & Vahid Dastjerdi, H. (2014). Investigating the effects of explicit and implicit instruction on Iranian EFL learners' pragmatic development: Speech acts of request and suggestion in focus. *International Journal of Research Studies in Language Learning, 3*(7), 1–12.

Saadatmandi, M., Khiabani, S. M., & Pourdana, N. (2018). Teaching English pragmatic features in EFL context: A focus on request speech acts. *Theory and Practice in Language Studies, 8*(7), 829–835.

Sabzalipour, B., & Koosha, M. (2016). The effect of using colligational corpus-based instruction on enhancing the pragmalinguistic knowledge of speech act of apology among Iranian intermediate EFL learners. *Modern Journal of Language Teaching Methods, 6*(9), 191–202.

Sadeqi, H., & Ghaemi, H. (2016). The effect of employing explicit pragmatics awareness-raising instruction on advanced EFL learner's use of politeness strategy of request via emails. *Modern Journal of Language Teaching Methods, 6*(1), 62–80.

Salehi, M. (2011). The effect of explicit versus implicit instruction: A case for apology and request speech acts. *International Conference on Languages, Literature and Linguistics IPEDR, 26*, 467–470.

Shakki, F., Naeini, J., Mazandarani, O., & Derakhshan, A. (2020). Instructed second language English pragmatics in the Iranian context. *Journal of Teaching Language Skills, 39*(1), 201–252. https://doi.org/10.22099/jtls.2020.38481.2886

Shakki, F., Neaini, J., Mazandarani, O., & Derakhshan, A. (2023). A meta-analysis on the instructed second language pragmatics for the speech acts of apology, request, and refusal in an Iranian EFL context. *Language Related Research, 13*(6), 461–510.

Shirinbakhsh, S., Rasekh, A. E., & Tavakoli, M. (2018). Metapragmatic instruction (6Rs) versus input-based practice: a comparison of their effects on pragmatic accuracy and speed in the recognition and oral production of English refusals. *The Language Learning Journal, 46*(4), 514–537.

Soler, E. A., & Pitarch, J. G. (2010). The effect of instruction on learners' pragmatic awareness: A focus on refusals. *International Journal of English Studies, 10*(1), 65–80.

Taguchi, N., & Kim, Y. (2016). Collaborative dialogue in learning pragmatics: Pragmatic-related episodes as an opportunity for learning request-making. *Applied Linguistics, 37*(3), 416–437.

Tajeddin, Z., & Bagherkazemi, M. (2014). Short-term and long-term impacts of individual and collaborative pragmatic output on speech act production. *Teaching English Language, 8*(1), 141–166.

Tajeddin, Z., & Hosseinpur, R. (2014a). The impact of deductive, inductive, and L1-based consciousness-raising tasks on EFL learners' acquisition of the request speech act. *Journal of Teaching Language Skills, 33*(1), 73–92.

Tajeddin, Z., & Hosseinpur, R. M. (2014b). The role of consciousness-raising tasks on EFL learners' microgenetic development of request pragmatic knowledge. *Iranian Journal of Applied Linguistics (IJAL), 17*(1), 187–147.

Tajeddin, Z., Keshavarz, M. H., & Zand-Moghadam, A. (2012). The effect of task-based language teaching on EFL learners' pragmatic production, metapragmatic awareness, and pragmatic self-assessment. *Iranian Journal of Applied Linguistics, 15*(2), 139–166.

Tanaka, H., & Oki, N. (2015). An attempt to raise Japanese EFL learners' pragmatic awareness using online discourse completion tasks. *JALT CALL Journal, 11*(2), 143–154.

References

Usó-Juan, E. (2022). Exploring the role of strategy instruction on learners' ability to write authentic email requests to faculty. *Language Teaching Research, 26*(2), 213–237.

Xiao-Le, G. (2011). The effect of explicit and implicit instructions of request strategies. *Intercultural Communication Studies, 20*(1), 104–123.

Zand-Moghadam, A., & Samani, F. M. (2021). Effect of information-gap, reasoning-gap, and opinion-gap tasks on EFL learners' pragmatic production, metapragmatic awareness, and comprehension of implicature. *TESL-EJ, 25*(1).

Zangoei, A., Nourmohammadi, E., & Derakhshan, A. (2014). The effect of consciousness-raising listening prompts on the development of the speech act of apology in an Iranian EFL context. *SAGE, 4*(2). https://doi.org/10.1177/2158244014531770

Ziafar, M. (2020). The influence of explicit, implicit, and contrastive lexical approaches on pragmatic competence: The case of Iranian EFL learners. *International Review of Applied Linguistics in Language Teaching, 58*(1), 103–131.

Ziashahabi, S., Jabbari, A. A., & Razmi, M. H. (2020). The effect of interventionist instructions of English conversational implicatures on Iranian EFL intermediate level learners' pragmatic competence development. *Cogent Education, 7*(1), 1–20. https://doi.org/10.1080/2331186X.2020.1840008

Chapter 5
Discussion

5.1 Introduction

After Kasper's plenary talk on the effectiveness of instruction (1996), a couple of review and meta-analysis studies were conducted on ISLA. And after Kasper and Rose's (2002) study found the importance of instruction in pragmatics, other researchers commenced investigating the effectiveness of instruction on L2 pragmatics (Bardovi-Harlig, 1996; Birjandi & Derakhshan, 2014; Blyth & Sykes, 2020; Cohen, 2020; Culpeper et al., 2018; González-Lloret, 2008; Kasper & Rose, 1999, 2002; Shakki et al., 2020, 2023; Taguchi, 2011, 2015, 2019; Takahashi, 2010a, 2010b). These studies reported that all features and norms of pragmatics, such as speech functions, address markers, and speech acts, are amenable to instruction. This postulation was endorsed by many scholars (Bardovi-Harlig, 2001, 2018; Bardovi-Harlig & Vellenga, 2012; Hassaskhah & Ebrahimi, 2015, Kaivanpanah & Langari, 2020; Khatib & Ahmadi Safa, 2001; Samavarchi & Allami, 2012; Tajeddin et al., 2012) and is further supported by the findings of the present study.

Request, apology, and refusal are recognized as the most researched speech acts. They are face-saving speech acts that play a special role in human life and aim to maintain harmony between interlocutors (Shakki et al., 2020). While plenty of research on the instruction targeting these speech acts has highlighted and recommended the advantages of teaching them (Taguchi, 2015), there has been no meta-analysis on the effectiveness of L2 pragmatic instruction for the speech acts of request, apology, and refusal together. Therefore, the present findings are justified by the only meta-analyses done by Derakhshan and Shakki (2021) and studies by Shakki et al. (2023) on the effectiveness of instruction of the speech act of request in an Iranian EFL context and the instruction of pragmatics in general as well as the results of other studies on teaching these speech acts. With respect to the learners' pragmatic knowledge, the findings of the present study lend support to Sharwood Smith's (1981, 1993) consciousness-raising and Schmidt's (1993) noticing hypothesis since it was found that instruction played a vital role in learners' awareness and boosted the process of learning. The findings of the current study are also supported by Bialystok (1993, 2011), who believes that implicit instruction should be analyzed and transformed into explicit instruction, which needs to be taught to be established.

5.2 Research Question 1: What is the Overall Effectiveness of the Instruction of L2 Pragmatics, Particularly the Speech Acts of Request, Apology, and Refusal?

Considering the interpretation of the effect sizes in SLA, as a field-specific benchmark, a d value of 0.60 is considered small, 1.00 is medium, and 1.40 is large (Plonsky & Oswald, 2014). In this study, the overall effect size was found to be $g = 1.72$, which is quite large and significant, corroborating the effectiveness of L2 pragmatic instruction. With regard to the speech acts of request, apology, and refusal, it was revealed that they lend themselves moderately to instruction with d values (Hedge's g) for the mentioned speech acts of $g = 1.34$, $g = 1.39$, and $g = 2.21$, respectively, demonstrating effect sizes are significant, medium, and large.

Similar to our findings, a recent meta-analysis conducted in the Iranian context by Shakki et al. (2023) reported that the overall effectiveness of pragmatic instruction for the instruction of the speech acts of request, apology, and refusal is $g = 1.43$, which shows L2 pragmatic instruction for the mentioned speech acts is efficient. They reported the following effect sizes, $g = 1.31$, $g = 1.35$, and $g = 0.98$ for request, apology, and refusal. As can be seen, there is no significant difference between the effect sizes of request and apology in the present study and the meta-analysis done in the Iranian context; however, the effectiveness of the speech act of refusal in the present study displayed a significant increase from Shakki et al.'s (2023) study.

By the same token, Ren et al. (2022) found an effect size of $g = 1.65$ for the overall effectiveness of L2 pragmatic instruction, which is a slight difference between our results and their findings. Their study used 29 primary studies with 54 generated effect sizes from the effects from all instructional types when a between-group comparison is used, and the data is associated with the immediate posttests. The large effect size reported in their study can elucidate the efficiency of pragmatic instruction. In line with our findings, Shakki et al. (2021) reported an effect size of $g = 1.34$ for the overall effectiveness of apology instruction of L2 pragmatics. Their results do not show any notable difference from the present study's findings, and it is immediately apparent that both studies accentuate the importance of L2 pragmatic instruction. They used 12 primary studies, and out of 12 generated effect sizes, a large and significant effect size was produced.

Our results show similarities with Derakhshan and Shakki's (2021) study in which the speech act of request was scrutinized. Their meta-analysis used 10 primary studies and generated 17 effect sizes. The effect size found for the overall effectiveness of L2 pragmatics instruction for the speech act of request was $g = 1.48$, which is quite large and significant. Similar to the results of our study, the instruction of L2 pragmatics

5.2 Research Question 1: What is the Overall Effectiveness …

was found to be efficient and therefore recommended. The present findings are also similar to Yousefi and Nassaji (2019) in that they both produced large and significant effect sizes for the overall effectiveness of pragmatic instruction. The effect size generated in this study was $d = 1.10$, and surprisingly it was larger in computer-mediated instruction than in face-to-face instruction. Generally, it can be concluded that instruction can contribute to better L2 pragmatic learning, and it is a prerequisite for language classes.

The importance of instruction for L2 pragmatics was highlighted in this study, as it was in Plonsky and Zhuang's (2019) research. They reported an effect of $d = 1.52$ for the overall effectiveness of pragmatic instruction, which is quite large and corroborates the teachability of pragmatics. This effect size closely resembled our findings and lent support to what was found in the current study. Correspondingly, Jeon and Kaya (2006), the first meta-analysis on the effectiveness of L2 pragmatic instruction, used 13 primary studies to conduct their research and reported an effect size of $d = 1.57$, which is large and significant. Their findings also verify the results in the present study, and both studies claim that instruction can be beneficial and efficient in L2 pragmatics learning.

Analyzing the previous meta-analyses on the effectiveness of L2 pragmatics revealed that all the conducted studies reported a large effect size that accentuates the importance of having instruction for teaching pragmatics as a second language. Overall, among the effect sizes reported so far, the lowest effect size is $d = 1.10$ in Yousefi and Nassaji (2019), and the highest is $g = 1.72$, generated by the present study. As a final point, it is interesting to note that all the effect sizes found for the effectiveness of L2 pragmatics are practically the same, confirming that instruction is pivotal and necessary. In a nutshell, it is clear that those students receiving L2 pragmatic instruction outperformed those who did not receive instruction (Fig. 5.1).

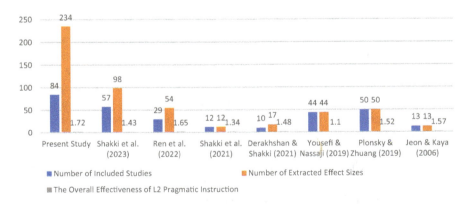

Fig. 5.1 An overview of the effectiveness of L2 pragmatics instruction for the last 22 years

5.3 Research Question 2: What are the Variables Which Moderate the Effectiveness of L2 Pragmatic Instruction, Especially the Speech Acts of Request, Apology, and Refusal?

The second research question scrutinized the moderating variables for the instruction of the speech acts of request, apology, and refusal in L2 pragmatics. An independent meta-regression analysis was conducted for each group of moderator variables to answer this question. In addition, Q-Statistic was used to evaluate if a particular variable was a significant moderator. The results of the meta-regression moderator analyses are presented in the previous chapter.

After considering demographic features such as age, gender, and proficiency level of the participants, it was revealed that age is a significant moderator for the instruction of L2 pragmatics, and specifically, the mixed age group was reported to have a higher effect size than the other age groups. Interestingly, gender was also a significant variable in pragmatic instruction, and among the studies analyzed, the studies in which gender was not explicitly mentioned generated the highest effect size. Moreover, the studies in which both genders were reported produced a larger effect size than research on female genders. The last feature, the participant's proficiency level, was another significant moderator in this meta-analysis. It was demonstrated that those participants with an upper-intermediate proficiency level produced a larger effect than other proficiency groups.

In addition to the demographic features, several design-related features were analyzed to determine whether they could be a moderating variable for the instruction of L2 pragmatics. The first variable was the design of the studies, which was not found to be a predictive or significant moderator for the effectiveness of pragmatic instruction. The second variable was the outcome measure, which was a significant moderator, with WDCTs reported to have a higher effect size than other measure groups. The psycholinguistic features of production and comprehension were both significant, with production generating a larger effect size than comprehension. The fourth variable was the treatment type which was reported to be a significant variable. Among different types of treatment, the explicit group produced a larger effect size than other groups. The final variable was the type of speech act, which was another significant moderator in L2 pragmatic instruction, with the speech act of refusal producing the largest effect size.

Ren et al.'s (2022) study reported similar results for the treatment type moderators (labeled as the teaching approach in their study); they also found that the superiority of explicit instruction over implicit one was inevitable and obvious. Similarly, both studies generated a larger effect size for the explicit group than the implicit group, though there was no significant difference between them. Another moderator shared by both studies was the proficiency level, and Ren et al. (2022) and the present study revealed that the intermediate levels generated a larger effect size than other proficiency Finally, after analyzing the psycholinguistic features, coded as pragmatic sub-competence in their study, Ren et al. (2022) reported a larger effect size for the

5.3 Research Question 2: What are the Variables Which Moderate …

perception or comprehension rather than the production of the pragmatics, in contrast to our findings.

As opposed to our finding that design is not a significant moderator for L2 pragmatic instruction, Shakki et al. (2021) found the design of the studies a predictive moderator for the instruction of apology. While treatment type was found to be a significant variable in this study, Shakki et al. (2021) claimed that treatment type is not a significant and predictive moderator for the instruction of apology in that context. Gender was also found to be a significant variable in this study. Interestingly, the studies in which gender was not reported generated a larger effect size than other gender groups, except Derakhshan and Shakki (2021), who found the male group more significant with a larger effect size. Unlike our results in which the male group produced an effect size of $g = 1.38$, in their study, the male group yielded an effect size of $g = 3.09$. Similar to our results, they reported the treatment type as a significant moderator, with the explicit group generating a larger effect size than the implicit one.

By the same token, Yousefi and Nassaji (2019) found a larger effect size for the explicit instruction than the implicit one, in agreement with our findings. Along with Ren et al. (2022), they also reported a larger effect size for comprehension compared to production, in contrast to our findings. They called the outcome measures task types and categorized them as selected responses, discourse completion tests, and free structured tasks. Similar to our findings, they found the effect size of discourse completion tests larger than other tests. Regarding the proficiency level of the participants, like the present study, they reported that L2 pragmatic instruction was most advantageous for intermediate-level students rather than advanced and beginners.

Regarding the instructional features, the results of the present study support the findings of Plonsky and Zhuang (2019) in that explicit instruction was more effective than implicit instruction. This fact was emphasized in both the previous meta-analyses and the systematic reviews conducted so far (Shakki et al., 2020; Taguchi, 2015). However, our current results are contrary to the findings of Plonsky and Zhuang (2019) on the effect of outcome measures. They found that controlled outcome measures such as WDCTs yielded a larger effect size than the free outcome measures like role play (Derakhshan & Shakki, 2021 on the speech act of request; Lee et al., (2015) on pronunciation instruction; Norris and Ortega (2000) on grammar instruction; Shakki et al., (2021) on the speech act of apology), although Plonsky and Zhuang (2019) reported a larger effect size for the free outcome measures like role plays than MDCTs and WDCTs.

With regard to the treatment type variable, Jeon and Kaya (2006) found that for experimental versus control group studies, Cohen's d was 0.70 for explicit teaching and $d = 0.44$ for implicit instruction. Considering pretest and posttest groups, again, the explicit instruction generated a larger effect size ($d = 1.90$) than the implicit one ($d = 1.01$). These results show that this study's findings align with the first meta-analysis conducted 17 years ago on 13 primary studies on the effectiveness of pragmatic instruction.

The superiority of L2 pragmatic instruction was justified through the analyses and reported findings, which concomitantly highlighted the positive effects of teaching the speech acts of request, apology, and refusal to learners. On par with our findings, the previous meta-analyses, Ren et al. (2022), Derakhshan and Shakki (2021), Shakki et al. (2021), Yousefi and Nassaji (2019), Plonsky and Zhuang (2019), Badjadi (2016), and Jeon and Kaya (2006) also corroborated the effectiveness of L2 pragmatic instruction, while also founding variables as moderators and predictors of pragmatic instruction.

References

Badjadi, N. E. I. (2016). A meta-analysis of the effects of instructional tasks on L2 pragmatics comprehension and production. In S. F. Tang & L. Logonnathan (Eds.), *Assessment for learning within and beyond the classroom* (pp. 241–268). Springer.

Bardovi-Harlig, K. (1996). Pragmatics and language teaching: Bringing pragmatics and pedagogy together. In L. Bouton (Ed.), *Pragmatics and language learning* (pp. 21–39). University of Illinois, Division of English as an International Language.

Bardovi-Harlig, K. (2001). Evaluating the empirical evidence: Grounds for instruction in pragmatics? In K. R. Rose & G. Kasper (Eds.), *Pragmatics in language teaching* (pp. 13–32). Cambridge.

Bardovi-Harlig, K. (2018). Matching modality in L2 pragmatics research design. *System, 75*, 13–22.

Bardovi-Harlig, K., & Vellenga, H. E. (2012). The effect of instruction on conventional expressions in L2 pragmatics. *System, 40*(1), 77–89.

Bialystok, E. (1993). Symbolic representation and attentional control. In G. Kasper & S. Blum-Kulka (Eds.), *Interlanguage pragmatics* (pp. 43–57). Oxford University Press.

Bialystok, E. (2011). How analysis and control lead to advantages and disadvantages in bilingual processing. In C. Sanz & R. P. Leow (Eds.), *Implicit and explicit conditions, processes and knowledge in SLA and bilingualism* (pp. 49–58). Georgetown University Press.

Birjandi, P., & Derakhshan, A. (2014). Pragmatic comprehension of apology, request, and refusal: An investigation on the effect of consciousness-raising video-driven prompts. *Applied Research on English Language, 3*(1), 67–85.

Blyth, C., & Sykes, J. (2020). Technology-enhanced L2 instructional pragmatics. *Language Learning & Technology, 24*(2), 1–7.

Cohen, A. D. (2020). Considerations in assessing pragmatic appropriateness in spoken language. *Language Teaching, 53*(2), 183–202.

Culpeper, J., Mackey, A., & Taguchi, N. (2018). *Second language pragmatics: From theory to research.* Routledge.

Derakhshan, A., & Shakki, F. (2021). A meta-analytic study of instructed second language pragmatics: A case of the speech act of request. *Journal of Research in Applied Linguistics, 12*(1), 15–32. https://doi.org/10.22055/RALS.2021.16722

González-Lloret, M. (2008). Computer-mediated learning of L2 pragmatics. In E. Alcón-Soler & A. Martı́nez-Flor (Eds). *Investigating pragmatics in foreign language learning, teaching and testing* (pp. 114–132). Multilingual Matters.

Hassaskhah, J., & Ebrahimi, H. (2015). A study of EFL learners' (meta) pragmatic learning through explicit (teacher explanation) and implicit (foreign film) interventions: The case of compliment. *Journal of Language Teaching and Research, 6*(2), 292–301.

Jeon, E. H., & Kaya, T. (2006). Effects of L2 instruction on interlanguage pragmatic development. In N. John & L. Ortega (Eds.), *Synthesizing research on language learning and teaching* (pp. 165–211). John Benjamins.

References

Kaivanpanah, S., & Langari, M. T. (2020). The effect of Bloom-based activities and Vygotskian scaffolding on Iranian EFL learners' use of the speech act of request. *Current Psychology.* https://doi.org/10.1007/s12144-020-01053-z

Kasper, G. (1996). Introduction: Interlanguage pragmatics in SLA. *Studies in Second Language Acquisition, 18*(2), 145–148.

Kasper, G., & Rose, K. R. (1999). Pragmatics and SLA. *Annual Review of Applied Linguistics, 19,* 81–104.

Kasper, G., & Rose, K. R. (2002). Pragmatic development in a second language. *Language Learning: A Journal of Research in Language Studies, 52*(1), 1–362.

Khatib, M., & Ahmadi Safa, M. (2001). The effectiveness of ZPD-wise explicit/implicit expert peers and coequals' scaffolding in ILP development. *Iranian Journal of Applied Linguistics, 14,* 49–75.

Norris, J. M., & Ortega, L. (2000). Effectiveness of L2 instruction: A research synthesis and quantitative meta-analysis. *Language Learning, 50*(3), 417–528. https://doi.org/10.1111/0023-8333.00136

Plonsky, L., & Oswald, F. L. (2014). How big is "big"? Interpreting effect sizes in l2 research. *Language Learning, 64*(4), 878–912. https://doi.org/10.1111/lang.12079

Plonsky, L., & Zhuang, J. (2019). A meta-analysis of L2 pragmatics instruction. In N. Taguchi (Ed.), *The Routledge handbook of SLA and pragmatics* (pp. 287–307). Routledge.

Ren, W., Li, S., & Lü, X. (2022). A meta-analysis of the effectiveness of second language pragmatics instruction. *Applied Linguistics, 1–21.* https://doi.org/10.1093/applin/amac055

Samavarchi, L., & Allami, H. (2012). Giving condolences by Persian EFL learners: A contrastive sociopragmatic study. *International Journal of English Linguistics, 2*(1), 71–78.

Schmidt, R. (1993). Consciousness, learning and interlanguage pragmatics. In G. Kasper & S. Blum- (Eds.), *Interlanguage pragmatics* (pp. 21–42). Oxford University Press.

Shakki, F., Naeini, J., Mazandarani, O., & Derakhshan, A. (2020). Instructed second language English pragmatics in the Iranian context. *Journal of Teaching Language Skills, 39*(1), 201–252. https://doi.org/10.22099/jtls.2020.38481.2886

Shakki, F., Naeini, J., Mazandarani, O., & Derakhshan, A. (2021). Instructed second language pragmatics for the speech act of apology in an Iranian EFL context: A meta-analysis. *Applied Research on English Language, 10*(3), 77–104.

Shakki, F., Neaini, J., Mazandarani, O., & Derakhshan, A. (2023). A meta-analysis on the instructed second language pragmatics for the speech acts of apology, request, and refusal in an Iranian EFL context. *Language Related Research, 13*(6), 461–510.

Sharwood Smith, M. (1981). Consciousness-raising and the second language learner. *Applied Linguistics, 2*(2), 159–168.

Sharwood Smith, M. (1993). Input enhancement in instructed second language acquisition: Theoretical bases. *Studies in Second Language Acquisition, 15*(2), 165–180.

Taguchi, N. (2011). Teaching pragmatics: Trends and issues. *Annual Review of Applied Linguistics, 31,* 289–310.

Taguchi, N. (2015). Instructed pragmatics at a glance: Where instructional studies were, are, and should be going. *Language Teaching, 48*(1), 1–50.

Taguchi, N. (Ed.). (2019). *The Routledge handbook of second language acquisition and pragmatics.* Routledge.

Tajeddin, Z., Keshavarz, M. H., & Zand-Moghadam, A. (2012). The effect of task-based language teaching on EFL learners' pragmatic production, metapragmatic awareness, and pragmatic self-assessment. *Iranian Journal of Applied Linguistics, 15*(2), 139–166.

Takahashi, S. (2010a). Assessing learnability in second language pragmatics. In A. Trosborg (Ed.), *Handbook of pragmatics* (pp. 391–421). Mouton de Gruyter.

Takahashi, S. (2010b). The effect of pragmatic instruction on speech act performance. In A. Martínez-Flor & E. Use-Juan (Eds.), *Speech act performance: Theoretical, empirical and methodological issues* (pp. 127–144). John Benjamins.

Yousefi, M., & Nassaji, H. (2019). A meta-analysis of the effects of instruction and corrective feedback on L2 pragmatics and the role of moderator variables: Face-to-face vs. computer-mediated instruction. *ITL-International Journal of Applied Linguistics, 170*(2), 277–308. https://doi.org/10.1075/itl.19012.you

Chapter 6
Conclusions, Limitations, Pedagogical Implications, and Directions for Future Research

6.1 Introduction

Pragmatic instruction appears to be complicated and challenging as pragmatic behavior changes to a large extent depending on the sociocultural contexts (Kondo, 2008). Although pragmatic features have been instructed in different EFL contexts for quite a while, the effectiveness of instruction in this field of study has not been scrutinized on a large scale. The results of the present meta-analysis corroborated the effectiveness of teaching speech acts of request, apology, and refusal. Moreover, moderator variables, such as age, gender, proficiency level, treatment types, speech acts, and outcome measures, were recognized as predictors of this effectiveness. Conducting this study provides a basis for some implications and suggestions for the researchers whose area of interest is L2 pragmatics. To this end, this chapter deals with a summary of the findings, the study's implications, and some suggestions for further research on ILP.

6.2 Limitations

Each and every study suffers from limitations, and this meta-analysis is no exception. Due to the fact that the soundness of meta-analyses relies on the original studies included in the study, some inevitable shortcomings and drawbacks mirroring the primary studies may exist. The limitations of this study are as follows:

(1) The first limitation is the number of studies used in the present study. The presence of publication bias indicates that more research needs to be done on the effect of teaching the speech acts of request, apology, and refusal, with only 84 studies meeting our coding criteria to be used in this book

(2) Inasmuch as not all of the studies reported age, gender, proficiency, assessment types, and language background in detail, there was missing data that caused several studies to be labeled as not reported, which may lead to inconclusive results.
(3) The dearth of research on other speech acts like compliments, complaints, etc., resulted in the focus of this study being solely on three frequent speech acts, request, apology, and refusal.
(4) The present study was limited to variables previously selected by the original study authors, and adding other variables may bring more original studies to the corpus.
(5) Another pivotal limitation was the number of words used in this meta-analysis. The fact that it was the first meta-analysis on the effectiveness of these speech acts worldwide limited the amount of literature to be discussed. Moreover, the lack of instruments, appendices, and questionnaires weakened this issue.

6.3 Implications

Overall, the findings of the present study indicated that learners not only need to learn the vocabulary and grammar of a target language, but they also need to be aware of the pragmatic features of that language to have meaningful communication. Due to the importance of pragmatic instruction, research on the effectiveness of L2 pragmatics has expanded in the last decades. The present meta-analysis analyzed 84 primary studies on the instruction of the speech acts of request, apology, and refusal. The studies were collected from 2000 to 2022 (when the book was written) and analyzed using CMA software. Reiterating Kasper and Rose's question on the teachability of pragmatics (2002), the present study found that pragmatic features are indeed teachable and explicit instruction is much more efficient than implicit teaching. Instruction can ameliorate the process of pragmatic acquisition, and it may sensitize the learners' metapragmatic knowledge, which is believed to be a prerequisite for pragmatic development (Takahashi, 2010).

To the best of our knowledge, this study investigated factors not yet explored and is the first research on the effectiveness of the instruction of request, apology, and refusal; therefore, the results may have pivotal pedagogical implications for L2 pragmatics instruction and future studies. One implication of this study came while searching for studies on speech acts; surprisingly, some speech acts, such as thanking, suggestions, complaints, condolences, threats, and congratulations, have received scant attention; accordingly, we recommend future researchers explore these untouched areas of English pragmatic instruction in their studies. A second implication is that the teachers should utilize the most effective treatment types, which would lead to better performance, comprehension, and production. They also should pay attention to other factors such as context, cultural background, and age of the learners to have better outcomes.

The present study's findings may be useful for researchers of pragmatics; in particular, the study of speech acts should check the moderator variables, which proved to be helpful and a predictor in teaching the speech act of request, apology, and refusal. Another important implication is including other data collection methods than WDCT and MDCT, such as role-play to get more reliable findings for the instruction of the mentioned speech acts, and including other commonly used teaching methods besides explicit and implicit such as meta-pragmatic activities, discussion, and input enhancement in their future studies. The final implication of the present book is to focus on different proficiency levels, especially making beginners aware of pragmatic knowledge as early as possible. Another implication is that most of the participants in L2 pragmatic studies are females, so it is a new area of research for the researchers to focus on males to check instruction effectiveness on this gender in L2 pragmatics.

6.4 Directions for Future Research

This study reiterated that L2 pragmatic instruction could be really efficient, and many studies have proved its effectiveness. Additionally, several variables were reported to be moderators of this effectiveness. Taking the results into account, some patterns and trends were elucidated, and the following directions are proposed for future research in this field of study. First, since the context of the primary studies was not the authors' concern or among the coding variables in the present meta-analysis, we recommend that future meta-analyses take contexts and cultural backgrounds into account. Besides the variety of contexts, various cultural backgrounds can be used as pivotal factors for the participants of future studies. Second, most effect sizes were generated for the above 18 age group, showing that adults or higher education students dominated participants of previous studies. Therefore, it is recommended to use a variety of ages in future studies to see whether pragmatic instruction is helpful for all age groups. Third, considering Kecskes' (2014) postulations that some shared knowledge, commonalities, and similar conventions and beliefs among the interlocuters are necessary to have a standard pragmatic communication, new studies are recommended in which intercultural communication is highlighted to avoid misunderstanding. Fourth, teaching English pragmatics to EFL learners is usually much easier than for students with nonEnglis-related majors such as art, political science, or engineering due to their exposure to features of speech acts, which make them cognizant of pragmatic features. One of the areas receiving scant attention is the instruction of L2 pragmatics to non-English major students. Future studies could focus on teaching different speech acts to students from other fields of study to check whether it is helpful. After analyzing the previous studies in L2 pragmatic instruction, it was revealed that qualitative design had been ignored in many contexts, and future research should focus on qualitative rather than quantitative design (with pretest, posttest, and control) to broaden the scope of English pragmatic instruction.

Fifth, scrutinizing previous studies showed that technology could be used more in pragmatic-related studies since pragmatic competence is one of the most vital constituents of communicative competence, which is rooted in current technology and communication (Taguchi & Sykes, 2013). For example, technology can be used as a coding variable for future meta-analyses to see its effectiveness. Last but not least, the ability to generalize a study's findings to actual situations is defined as ecological validity (Derakhshan & Shakki, 2020), which should be considered an essential factor for future research. When a study pays attention to ecological validity, the applicability of the results can be reported and evidenced. Real-life class situations must be used in research to form an inextricable relationship with culture and the educational system. Finally, researchers must relinquish control of the classes in their studies since the more they control the situation, the less ecological validity is achieved; therefore, genuine engagement and teachers' support and rapport are recommended in L2 pragmatic instruction studies (Al-Obaydi et al., 2023; Shakki, 2022a; Thorne, 2013).

6.5 Conclusions

A remarkable shift in second language acquisition and applied pragmatics has occurred in recent decades. Pragmatic competence, knowledge about norms and conventions of a language, and language skills must gain remarkable momentum to nullify pragmatic failure. Pragmatic competence should be highlighted and practiced in line with the knowledge and skills to avoid misunderstanding. Boosting pragmatics knowledge requires instruction, and teaching pragmatic features can benefit language learners (Cohen & Ishihara, 2013; Derakhshan & Eslami, 2015; Félix-Brasdefer, 2008; Shakki et al., 2020, 2021, 2023; Taguchi, 2015; Takahashi, 2015).

Among research methods, meta-analyses have shown superiority in recent years (Norris & Ortega, 2000), and an amalgamation of studies has been done on the effect of instruction in L2 pragmatics (Badjadi, 2016; Derakhshan & Shakki, 2021; Jeon & Kaya, 2006; Plonsky & Zhuang, 2019; Shakki et al., 2021, 2023; Yousefi & Nassaji, 2019). Considering the prominence of pragmatics, particularly the speech acts of request, apology, and refusal, the present meta-analysis was conducted to investigate the overall effectiveness of instruction of L2 pragmatics and the moderator variables involved in various contexts.

This meta-analysis presented a summative description of empirical studies conducted on the instruction of the speech acts of request, apology, and refusal worldwide during the last 22 years. The purpose of conducting this study was to fill the gap of no meta-analysis having been done on the effect of instruction of all three mentioned speech acts. Resonating with what Taguchi (2015), Yousefi and Nassaji (2019), and Derakhshan and Shakki (2021) stated, the present meta-analysis agrees with the previous studies on the effectiveness of L2 pragmatic instruction, revealing that the instruction of the speech acts of request, apology, and refusal has many benefits for learners in different contexts around the world.

The findings of this study also revealed that pragmatic instruction could be the panacea that ameliorates the hardships of meaningful communication. It is concluded that some moderator variables, such as age, gender, proficiency level, treatment types, speech acts, and outcome measures, can be predictors for pragmatic instruction. However, other moderators, such as the study design and psycholinguistic features, produced large effect sizes; hence, they cannot be a predictor for the instruction of request, apology, and refusal. Moreover, the results of this study demonstrated that the frequency of the mentioned speech acts is as follows: Request was used in 85 studies, Mixed speech acts in 65, Apology in 46, and Refusal in 38 studies. Similarly, WDCT dominated the outcome measures in this study with 142 studies, MDCT was used in 51, Mixed in 2, and Other outcome measures in 93 studies. Considering the treatment types, 103 studies conducted Explicit teaching, 26 used Implicit instruction, 2 used Mixed (explicit and implicit), and 103 studies used Other teaching methods in their research. Among the psycholinguistic features, Comprehension was investigated in 56 studies, even though it was superior, Production in 172 studies, and Mixed in 6 studies. Regarding the design of the study, 151 studies used Experimental, and 83 studies utilized Quasi-experimental in their analysis.

To check the participants' characteristics, the age moderator was divided into three groups, with 35 studies conducted on the Below-18 age group, 129 studies on the Above-18 age group, 25 studies on Both age groups, and 45 studies not reporting the age of the learners. Analyzing the level of proficiency, 56 studies used Pre-intermediate learners, 57 studies used Intermediate learners, 29 studies used Upper-intermediate participants, 16 studies were carried out on Advanced learners, 22 studies used Mixed proficiency levels, and 54 studies did not report the proficiency level of the participants. Regarding gender, 61 studies focused on Females, 8 on Males, 124 Mixed, and 41 studies did not mention the exact gender of the participants.

References

Al-Obaydi, L. H., Shakki, F., Tawafak, R. M., Pikhart, M., & Ugla, R. L. (2023). What I know, what I want to know, what I learned: Activating EFL college students' cognitive, behavioral, and emotional engagement through structured feedback in an online environment. *Frontiers in Psychology, 13*, 1083673. https://doi.org/10.3389/fpsyg.2022.1083673

Badjadi, N. E. I. (2016). A meta-analysis of the effects of instructional tasks on L2 pragmatics comprehension and production. In S. F. Tang & L. Logonnathan (Eds.), *Assessment for learning within and beyond the classroom* (pp. 241–268). Springer.

Cohen, A. D., & Ishihara, N. (2013). Pragmatics. In B. Tomlinson (Ed.), *Applied linguistics and materials development* (pp. 113–126). Bloomsbury.

Derakhshan, A., & Eslami, Z. R. (2015). The effect of consciousness-raising instruction on the comprehension of apology & request. *TESL-EJ, 18*(4). http://www.tesl-ej.org/wordpress/issues/volume18/ej72/ej72a6/

Derakhshan, A., & Shakki, F. (2020). Review of the book *Doing SLA research with implications for the classroom reconciling methodological demands and pedagogical applicability*, by R. M. DeKeyser and G. P. Botana. *International Journal of Applied Linguistics*. https://doi.org/10.1111/ijal.12290

Derakhshan, A., & Shakki, F. (2021). A meta-analytic study of instructed second language pragmatics: A case of the speech act of request. *Journal of Research in Applied Linguistics, 12*(1), 15–32. https://doi.org/10.22055/RALS.2021.16722

Félix-Brasdefer, J. C. (2008). Teaching pragmatics in the classroom: Instruction of mitigation in Spanish as a foreign language. *Hispania, 91*, 479–494.

Jeon, E. H., & Kaya, T. (2006). Effects of L2 instruction on interlanguage pragmatic development. In N. John & L. Ortega (Eds.), *Synthesizing research on language learning and teaching* (pp. 165–211). John Benjamins.

Kasper, G., & Rose, K. R. (2002). Pragmatic development in a second language. *Language Learning: A Journal of Research in Language Studies, 52*(1), 1–362.

Kecskes, I. (2014). *Intercultural pragmatics*. Oxford University Press.

Kondo, S. (2008). Effects on pragmatic development through awareness-raising instruction: Refusals by Japanese EFL learners. In E. Alcón-Soler & A. Martínez-Flor (Eds.), *Investigating pragmatics in foreign language learning, teaching and testing* (pp. 153–177). Multilingual Matters.

Norris, J. M., & Ortega, L. (2000). Effectiveness of L2 instruction: A research synthesis and quantitative meta-analysis. *Language Learning, 50*(3), 417–528. https://doi.org/10.1111/0023-8333.00136

Plonsky, L., & Zhuang, J. (2019). A meta-analysis of L2 pragmatics instruction. In N. Taguchi (Ed.), *The Routledge handbook of SLA and pragmatics* (pp. 287–307). Routledge.

Shakki, F. (2022a). Iranian EFL students' L2 engagement: The effects of teacher-student rapport and teacher support. *Language Related Research, 13*(3), 175–198. https://doi.org/10.52547/LRR.13.3.8

Shakki, F. (2022b). Meta-analysis as an emerging trend to scrutinize the effectiveness of L2 pragmatic instruction. *Frontiers in Psychology, 13*. https://doi.org/10.3389/fpsyg.2022.101666

Shakki, F., Naeini, J., Mazandarani, O., & Derakhshan, A. (2020). Instructed second language English pragmatics in the Iranian context. *Journal of Teaching Language Skills, 39*(1), 201–252. https://doi.org/10.22099/jtls.2020.38481.2886

Shakki, F., Naeini, J., Mazandarani, O., & Derakhshan, A. (2021). Instructed second language pragmatics for the speech act of apology in an Iranian EFL context: A meta-analysis. *Applied Research on English Language, 10*(3), 77–104.

Shakki, F., Neaini, J., Mazandarani, O., & Derakhshan, A. (2023). A meta-analysis on the instructed second language pragmatics for the speech acts of apology, request, and refusal in an Iranian EFL context. *Language Related Research, 13*(6), 461–510.

Taguchi, N. (2015). Instructed pragmatics at a glance: Where instructional studies were, are, and should be going. *Language Teaching, 48*(1), 1–50.

Taguchi, N., & Sykes, J. M. (2013). *Technology in interlanguage pragmatics research and teaching*. John Benjamins.

Takahashi, S. (2010). The effect of pragmatic instruction on speech act performance. In A. Martínez-Flor & E. Use-Juan (Eds.), *Speech act performance: Theoretical, empirical and methodological issues* (pp. 127–144). John Benjamins.

Takahashi, S. (2015). The effects of learner profiles on pragmalinguistic awareness and learning. *System, 48*, 48–61.

Thorne, S. L. (2013). Language learning, ecological validity, and innovation under conditions of superdiversity. *Bellaterra Journal of Teaching & Learning Language & Literature, 6*(2), 1–27.

Yousefi, M., & Nassaji, H. (2019). A meta-analysis of the effects of instruction and corrective feedback on L2 pragmatics and the role of moderator variables: Face-to-face vs. computer-mediated instruction. *ITL-International Journal of Applied Linguistics, 170*(2), 277–308. https://doi.org/10.1075/itl.19012.you

Appendix
Results for All Studies Included

Appendix: Results for All Studies Included

Study name	Subgroup	Outcome	Time point	Hedges' g	Std. error	Variance	Lower limit	Upper limit	Z-value	p-value
Abdullahizadeh et al. (2014)	M	MDCT	Posttest	2.3693	.3343	.1117	1.7142	3.0244	7.0883	.000
Ahmadi et al. (2011)	A	WDCT	Posttest	.8456	.2087	.0435	.4367	1.2546	4.0528	.000
Ahmadi et al. (2011)	B	WDCT	Delayed	.8456	.2087	.0435	.4367	1.2546	4.0528	.000
Ahmadi et al. (2011)	C	MDCT	Posttest	.8456	.2087	.0435	.4367	1.2546	4.0528	.000
Ahmadi et al. (2011)	D	MDCT	Delayed	.8456	.2087	.0435	.4367	1.2546	4.0528	.000
Ahmadian (2020)	A	WDCT	Posttest	4.7536	.5403	.2919	3.6947	5.8125	8.7985	.000
Ahmadian (2020)	B	WDCT	Posttest	3.7028	.4544	.2065	2.8123	4.5934	8.1493	.000
Ahmadian (2020)	C	WDCT	Delayed	4.8312	.5469	.2990	3.7594	5.9030	8.8345	.000
Ahmadian (2020)	D	WDCT	Delayed	3.4131	.4320	.1866	2.5664	4.2598	7.9005	.000
Ahmadian (2020)	E	MDCT	Posttest	.7048	.2818	.0794	.1526	1.2571	2.5014	.012
Ahmadian (2020)	F	MDCT	Posttest	1.6613	.3181	.1012	1.0380	2.2847	5.2234	.000
Ahmadian (2020)	G	MDCT	Delayed	1.9353	.3326	.1106	1.2834	2.5872	5.8184	.000
Ahmadian (2020)	H	MDCT	Delayed	.7873	.2839	.0806	.2309	1.3437	2.7734	.006
Alcon-Soler (2005)	A	WDCT	Posttest	6.8748	.6774	.4588	5.5472	8.2024	10.1495	.000
Alcon-Soler (2005)	B	WDCT	Delayed	3.4306	.4038	.1630	2.6392	4.2219	8.4966	.000
Alcon-Soler (2005)	C	WDCT	Post Delayed	−.2014	.2555	.0653	−.7022	.2994	−.7882	.431
Alcon-Soler (2010)	M	WDCT	Posttest	2.3443	.2014	.0406	1.9496	2.7391	11.6405	.000
Alcon-Soler (2015)	A	WDCT	Posttest	7.5512	.7349	.5401	6.1108	8.9916	10.2748	.000
Alcon-Soler (2015)	B	WDCT	Delayed	3.2694	.3925	.1540	2.5002	4.0386	8.3307	.000
Alcon-Soler (2015)	C	WDCT	Post Delayed	.1586	.2553	.0652	−.3417	.6589	.6214	.534
Alcon-Soler (2017)	A	WDCT	Posttest	7.3066	.7140	.5098	5.9071	8.7060	10.2330	.000
Alcon-Soler (2017)	B	WDCT	Posttest	6.8748	.6774	.4588	5.5472	8.2024	10.1495	.000

(continued)

Appendix: Results for All Studies Included

(continued)

Study name	Subgroup	Outcome	Time point	Hedges' g	Std. error	Variance	Lower limit	Upper limit	Z-value	p-value
Anani Sarab & Alikhani (2016a)	A	MDCT	Posttest	1.0366	.2675	.0716	.5123	1.5610	3.8747	.000
Anani Sarab & Alikhani (2016a)	B	WDCT	Posttest	1.1046	.2697	.0727	.5759	1.6332	4.0953	.000
Anani Sarab & Alikhani (2016b)	A	WDCT	Posttest	1.3752	.2796	.0782	.8273	1.9231	4.9190	.000
Anani Sarab & Alikhani (2016b)	B	MDCT	Posttest	1.0333	.2674	.0715	.5092	1.5575	3.8640	.000
Bagheri & Hmrang (2013)	A	MDCT	Posttest	2.0569	.3165	.1002	1.4365	2.6773	6.4979	.000
Bagheri & Hmrang (2013)	B	WDCT	Posttest	2.3700	.3343	.1118	1.7148	3.0252	7.0896	.000
Bagherkazemi & Harati (2022)	A	WDCT	Posttest	.3456	.2441	.0596	−.1327	.8240	1.4161	.157
Bagherkazemi & Harati (2022)	B	WDCT	Posttest	1.1896	.2612	.0682	.6778	1.7015	4.5552	.000
Bagherkazemi (2018)	M	WDCT	Posttest	1.0636	.2952	.0872	.4850	1.6422	3.6027	.000
Baindir (2019)	M	WDCT	Posttest	1.7439	.3961	.1569	.9676	2.5202	4.4030	.000
Barekat & Mehri (2013)	A	WDCT	Posttest	3.0007	.5256	.2763	1.9705	4.0309	5.7087	.000
Barekat & Mehri (2013)	B	WDCT	Posttest	4.1637	.6443	.4152	2.9008	5.4266	6.4620	.000
Bashang & Zenouzagh (2021)	M	WDCT	Posttest	2.7004	.3980	.1584	1.9204	3.4804	6.7856	.000
Bataine et al. (2017)	M	WDCT	Posttest	1.4175	.3248	.1055	.7808	2.0542	4.3637	.000
Birjandi & Derakhshan (2014)	A	MDCT	Posttest	2.4124	.4179	.1747	1.5932	3.2316	5.7721	.000

(continued)

(continued)

Study name	Subgroup	Outcome	Time point	Hedges' g	Std. error	Variance	Lower limit	Upper limit	Z-value	p-value
Birjandi & Derakhshan (2014)	B	MDCT	Posttest	1.5677	.3666	.1344	.8492	2.2861	4.2768	.000
Birjandi & Derakhshan (2014)	C	MDCT	Posttest	.7028	.3410	.1163	.0346	1.3711	2.0613	.039
Birjandi & Pezeshki (2012)	A	WDCT	Posttest	2.9251	.4308	.1856	2.0806	3.7695	6.7891	.000
Birjandi & Pezeshki (2012)	B	WDCT	Posttest	3.4652	.4961	.2462	2.4927	4.4376	6.9842	.000
Buftira et al. (2022)	A	MDCT	Posttest	1.7603	.2886	.0833	1.1948	2.3259	6.1005	.000
Buftira et al. (2022)	B	WDCT	Posttest	2.3293	.3494	.1220	1.6446	3.0140	6.6676	.000
Buftira et al. (2022)	C	Mixed	Posttest	3.2184	.4519	.2043	2.3326	4.1042	7.1213	.000
Canbolat et al. (2021)	M	MDCT	Posttest	.5363	.4181	.1748	−.2832	1.3557	1.2826	.200
Davarzani & Talebzade (2020)	A	MDCT	Posttest	.4480	.1965	.0386	.0628	.8332	2.2795	.023
Davarzani & Talebzade (2020)	B	MDCT	Posttest	.4479	.1965	.0386	.0627	.8331	2.2790	.023
Derakhshan & Arabmofrad (2018)	A	MDCT	Posttest	2.6748	.4679	.2189	1.7577	3.5919	5.7165	.000
Derakhshan & Arabmofrad (2018)	B	MDCT	Posttest	1.7627	.4042	.1634	.9704	2.5550	4.3605	.000
Derakhshan & Arabmofrad (2018)	C	MDCT	Posttest	.8388	.3609	.1302	.1315	1.5461	2.3243	.020
Derakhshan & Eslami (2015)	A	MDCT	Posttest	4.6449	.7651	.5854	3.1452	6.1445	6.0706	.000
Derakhshan & Eslami (2015)	B	MDCT	Posttest	5.6126	.9130	.8336	3.8231	7.4020	6.1473	.000

(continued)

Appendix: Results for All Studies Included

(continued)

Study name	Subgroup	Outcome	Time point	Hedges' g	Std. error	Variance	Lower limit	Upper limit	Z-value	p-value
Derakhshan & Eslami (2015)	C	MDCT	Posttest	5.1695	.8451	.7142	3.5132	6.8258	6.1171	.000
Derakhshan & Shakki (2020)	A	MDCT	Posttest	3.2525	.5251	.2758	2.2233	4.2818	6.1937	.000
Derakhshan & Shakki (2020)	B	MDCT	Posttest	2.2356	.4373	.1912	1.3786	3.0926	5.1126	.000
Djouani (2017)	M	MDCT	Posttest	.8865	.3108	.0966	.2774	1.4957	2.8524	.004
Duong (2016)	A	WDCT	Posttest	4.2642	.4243	.1800	3.4327	5.0958	10.0511	.000
Duong (2016)	B	WDCT	Posttest	4.5457	.4458	.1988	3.6719	5.4196	10.1959	.000
Duong (2016)	C	WDCT	Delayed	6.6233	.5926	.3512	5.4618	7.7849	11.1759	.000
Duong (2016)	D	WDCT	Delayed	7.3835	.6538	.4275	6.1020	8.6650	11.2926	.000
Eslami & Mardani (2010)	M	WDCT	Posttest	2.1044	.3191	.1018	1.4789	2.7299	6.5939	.000
Eslami, Eslami & Fatahi (2004)	M	WDCT	Posttest	1.3197	.2691	.0724	.7922	1.8472	4.9035	.000
Eslami, Mirzaei & Dini (2014)	A	WDCT	Posttest	3.1308	.4196	.1760	2.3085	3.9531	7.4623	.000
Eslami, Mirzaei & Dini (2014)	B	WDCT	Posttest	2.1660	.3497	.1223	1.4806	2.8515	6.1938	.000
Fakher Ajabshir & Panahifar (2020)	A	WDCT	Posttest	4.7897	.4655	.2167	3.8774	5.7021	10.2895	.000
Fakher Ajabshir & Panahifar (2020)	B	WDCT	Posttest	7.4151	.6390	.4084	6.1626	8.6676	11.6035	.000
Fakher Ajabshir (2018)	A	WDCT	Posttest	.1549	.2376	.0565	−.3108	.6207	.6519	.514
Fakher Ajabshir (2018)	B	WDCT	Posttest	.2261	.2410	.0581	−.2462	.6984	.9383	.348

(continued)

(continued)

Study name	Subgroup	Outcome	Time point	Hedges' g	Std. error	Variance	Lower limit	Upper limit	Z-value	p-value
Fakher Ajabshir (2022)	A	Other	Posttest	1.5769	.3775	.1425	.8370	2.3167	4.1776	.000
Fakher Ajabshir (2022)	B	Other	Posttest	.9334	.2977	.0886	.3499	1.5169	3.1352	.002
Fakher Ajabshir (2022)	C	Other	Posttest	.9239	.2801	.0785	.3749	1.4730	3.2985	.001
Fakher Ajabshir (2022)	D	WDCT	Posttest	1.6868	.3930	.1544	.9166	2.4571	4.2923	.000
Fakher Ajabshir (2022)	E	WDCT	Posttest	.5126	.2614	.0684	.0002	1.0251	1.9608	.050
Fakher Ajabshir (2022)	F	WDCT	Posttest	1.2173	.3113	.0969	.6071	1.8275	3.9098	.000
Farahian, Rezaei & Gholami (2012)	A	WDCT	Posttest	7.0287	.8954	.8017	5.2739	8.7836	7.8502	.000
Farahian, Rezaei & Gholami (2012)	B	WDCT	Delayed	6.9169	.8816	.7773	5.1889	8.6449	7.8454	.000
Fathi & Feizi (2018)	A	WDCT	Posttest	.7580	.2257	.0509	.3157	1.2003	3.3586	.001
Fathi & Feizi (2018)	B	WDCT	Posttest	1.0874	.2383	.0568	.6203	1.5546	4.5624	.000
Gaily (2014)	A	WDCT	Posttest	.8020	.2493	.0622	.3133	1.2906	3.2167	.001
Gaily (2014)	B	WDCT	Posttest	1.2088	.2874	.0826	.6454	1.7721	4.2056	.000
Gaily (2014)	C	WDCT	Posttest	.8754	.2554	.0652	.3748	1.3760	3.4273	.001
Gaily (2014)	D	WDCT	Posttest	.6524	.2382	.0567	.1856	1.1191	2.7392	.006
Gharibeh, Mirzaei & Yaghubi (2016)	M	WDCT	Posttest	1.4192	.1969	.0388	1.0333	1.8051	7.2078	.000
Haghighi et al. (2019)	M	WDCT	Posttest	1.2400	.2789	.0778	.6935	1.7866	4.4469	.000
Halenko & Florez (2020)	A	WDCT	Posttest	1.4822	.3913	.1531	.7153	2.2491	3.7880	.000
Halenko & Florez (2020)	B	WDCT	Posttest	.6545	.3542	.1255	-.0398	1.3487	1.8477	.065
Hernandez (2021)	M	Other	Posttest	2.4042	.6018	.3621	1.2248	3.5837	3.9953	.000
Hrrnandez & Boero (2017)	M	WDCT	Posttest	.1232	.2451	.0601	-.3573	.6037	.5027	.615

(continued)

Appendix: Results for All Studies Included

(continued)

Study name	Subgroup	Outcome	Time point	Hedges' g	Std. error	Variance	Lower limit	Upper limit	Z-value	p-value
Iraji et al. (2018)	M	MDCT	Posttest	1.5306	.3540	.1253	.8366	2.2245	4.3231	.000
Jesmin & Hamoudy (2009)	A	WDCT	Posttest	2.1544	.3843	.1477	1.4011	2.9077	5.6055	.000
Jesmin & Hamoudy (2009)	B	WDCT	Posttest	2.3683	.4120	.1697	1.5609	3.1757	5.7490	.000
Jesmin & Hamoudy (2009)	C	WDCT	Posttest	3.3718	.5483	.3006	2.2972	4.4464	6.1497	.000
Jesmin & Hamoudy (2009)	D	WDCT	Posttest	2.3891	.4147	.1719	1.5763	3.2018	5.7614	.000
Kachamat (2018)	M	WDCT	Posttest	3.3455	.5446	.2966	2.2780	4.4129	6.1429	.000
Kaivanpahah & Langari (2020)	A	WDCT	Posttest	3.7625	.5047	.2547	2.7734	4.7516	7.4555	.000
Kaivanpahah & Langari (2020)	B	WDCT	Delayed	3.3627	.4707	.2216	2.4401	4.2852	7.1441	.000
Kargar, Sadighi & Ahmadi (2012)	A	WDCT	Posttest	1.8392	.3185	.1014	1.2149	2.4635	5.7744	.000
Kargar, Sadighi & Ahmadi (2012)	B	WDCT	Posttest	1.4902	.2989	.0894	.9043	2.0761	4.9848	.000
Kargar, Sadighi & Ahmadi (2012)	C	WDCT	Posttest	1.9414	.3240	.1050	1.3064	2.5764	5.9924	.000
Kargar, Sadighi & Ahmadi (2012)	D	WDCT	Posttest	.0453	.2659	.0707	−.4759	.5665	.1702	.865
Kargar, Sadighi & Ahmadi (2012)	E	WDCT	Delayed	1.6789	.3104	.0963	1.0706	2.2871	5.4095	.000
Kargar, Sadighi & Ahmadi (2012)	F	WDCT	Delayed	1.7837	.3130	.0979	1.1703	2.3971	5.6994	.000
Kargar, Sadighi & Ahmadi (2012)	G	WDCT	Delayed	1.3125	.2939	.0864	.7365	1.8884	4.4663	.000

(continued)

(continued)

Study name	Subgroup	Outcome	Time point	Hedges' g	Std. error	Variance	Lower limit	Upper limit	Z-value	p-value
Kargar, Sadighi & Ahmadi (2012)	H	WDCT	Delayed	.5969	.2719	.0739	.0640	1.1299	2.1953	.028
Kargar, Sadighi & Ahmadi (2012)	I	Other	Posttest	1.9428	.3241	.1050	1.3077	2.5779	5.9953	.000
Kargar, Sadighi & Ahmadi (2012)	J	Other	Posttest	2.0324	.3319	.1102	1.3818	2.6830	6.1226	.000
Kargar, Sadighi & Ahmadi (2012)	K	Other	Posttest	2.0770	.3315	.1099	1.4272	2.7268	6.2649	.000
Kargar, Sadighi & Ahmadi (2012)	L	Other	Posttest	.4513	.2650	.0702	−.0681	.9708	1.7029	.089
Kargar, Sadighi & Ahmadi (2012)	N	Other	Delayed	2.1340	.3348	.1121	1.4778	2.7903	6.3739	.000
Kargar, Sadighi & Ahmadi (2012)	O	Other	Delayed	1.7027	.3143	.0988	1.0867	2.3187	5.4174	.000
Kargar, Sadighi & Ahmadi (2012)	P	Other	Delayed	.9192	.2800	.0784	.3704	1.4679	3.2832	.001
Kargar, Sadighi & Ahmadi (2012)	Q	Other	Delayed	.8008	.2722	.0741	.2673	1.3342	2.9421	.003
Kargar, Sadighi & Ahmadi (2012)	R	Other	Posttest	.9143	.2883	.0831	.3493	1.4793	3.1716	.002
Kargar, Sadighi & Ahmadi (2012)	S	Other	Posttest	.8700	.2870	.0823	.3075	1.4324	3.0317	.002
Kargar, Sadighi & Ahmadi (2012)	T	Other	Posttest	1.1471	.2987	.0892	.5617	1.7325	3.8408	.000

(continued)

Appendix: Results for All Studies Included

(continued)

Study name	Subgroup	Outcome	Time point	Hedges' g	Std. error	Variance	Lower limit	Upper limit	Z-value	p-value
Kargar, Sadighi & Ahmadi (2012)	U	Other	Posttest	.1282	.2765	.0765	−.4137	.6702	.4637	.643
Kargar, Sadighi & Ahmadi (2012)	V	Other	Delayed	1.0557	.2929	.0858	.4817	1.6298	3.6046	.000
Kargar, Sadighi & Ahmadi (2012)	W	Other	Delayed	1.2148	.2988	.0893	.6293	1.8004	4.0663	.000
Kargar, Sadighi & Ahmadi (2012)	X	Other	Delayed	.9778	.2927	.0857	.4041	1.5515	3.3406	.001
Kargar, Sadighi & Ahmadi (2012)	Y	Other	Delayed	.4300	.2795	.0781	−.1177	.9778	1.5387	.124
Khatib & Ahmadi Safa (2011)	A	MDCT	Posttest	.8661	.3332	.1110	.2130	1.5192	2.5992	.009
Khatib & Ahmadi Safa (2011)	B	MDCT	Posttest	1.0661	.3595	.1293	.3614	1.7707	2.9652	.003
Khatib & Ahmadi Safa (2011)	C	MDCT	Posttest	.3024	.3279	.1075	−.3402	.9451	.9225	.356
Khatib & Ahmadi Safa (2011)	D	WDCT	Posttest	2.0098	.3928	.1543	1.2398	2.7797	5.1161	.000
Khatib & Ahmadi Safa (2011)	E	WDCT	Posttest	1.6755	.3922	.1538	.9068	2.4442	4.2720	.000
Khatib & Ahmadi Safa (2011)	F	WDCT	Posttest	.7773	.3386	.1146	.1137	1.4408	2.2959	.022
Khodareza & Lotfi (2013)	A	MDCT	Posttest	2.2397	.3394	.1152	1.5744	2.9050	6.5982	.000
Khodareza & Lotfi (2013)	B	WDCT	Posttest	6.0273	.7982	.6371	4.4629	7.5917	7.5513	.000
Malaz et al. (2011)	A	WDCT	Posttest	.0005	.2441	.0596	−.4780	.4789	.0019	.998

(continued)

(continued)

Study name	Subgroup	Outcome	Time point	Hedges' g	Std. error	Variance	Lower limit	Upper limit	Z-value	p-value
Malaz et al. (2011)	B	WDCT	Posttest	.2224	.2475	.0612	−.2627	.7074	.8985	.369
Malaz et al. (2011)	C	WDCT	Posttest	.2224	.2475	.0612	−.2627	.7074	.8985	.369
Malaz et al. (2011)	D	WDCT	Posttest	.3352	.2517	.0633	−.1581	.8284	1.3317	.183
Malaz et al. (2011)	E	WDCT	Posttest	.1651	.2460	.0605	−.3170	.6472	.6711	.502
Malaz et al. (2011)	F	WDCT	Posttest	.3352	.2517	.0633	−.1581	.8284	1.3317	.183
Malaz et al. (2011)	G	WDCT	Posttest	.3352	.2517	.0633	−.1581	.8284	1.3317	.183
Malaz et al. (2011)	H	WDCT	Posttest	.4717	.2589	.0670	−.0356	.9791	1.8223	.068
Mirzaei & Esmaili (2013)	A	MDCT	Posttest	4.5933	.4907	.2408	3.6316	5.5550	9.3611	.000
Mirzaei & Esmaili (2013)	B	MDCT	Posttest	2.5824	.3472	.1205	1.9020	3.2629	7.4387	.000
Mirzaei & Esmaili (2013)	C	WDCT	Posttest	1.5896	.2933	.0860	1.0148	2.1643	5.4203	.000
Mirzaei & Esmaili (2013)	D	WDCT	Posttest	1.5805	.3251	.1057	.9433	2.2178	4.8610	.000
Mouna (2016)	M	Mixed	Posttest	1.4097	.2614	.0683	.8973	1.9220	5.3926	.000
Nemati & Arabmofrad (2014)	A	MDCT	Posttest	1.1664	.3724	.1387	.4364	1.8963	3.1319	.002
Nemati & Arabmofrad (2014)	B	MDCT	Posttest	1.6788	.4010	.1608	.8929	2.4647	4.1867	.000
Nemati & Arabmofrad (2014)	C	MDCT	Posttest	.7257	.3114	.0970	.1154	1.3361	2.3304	.020
Nemati & Arabmofrad (2014)	D	MDCT	Posttest	1.0357	.3391	.1150	.3711	1.7004	3.0541	.002
Nemati & Arabmofrad (2014)	E	WDCT	Posttest	3.5759	.5584	.3118	2.4814	4.6703	6.4037	.000

(continued)

Appendix: Results for All Studies Included

(continued)

Study name	Subgroup	Outcome	Time point	Hedges' g	Std. error	Variance	Lower limit	Upper limit	Z-value	p-value
Nemati & Arabmofrad (2014)	F	WDCT	Posttest	2.7434	.4818	.2321	1.7991	3.6877	5.6943	.000
Nemati & Arabmofrad (2014)	G	WDCT	Posttest	1.0999	.3239	.1049	.4650	1.7347	3.3954	.001
Nemati & Arabmofrad (2014)	H	WDCT	Posttest	1.8055	.3956	.1565	1.0301	2.5808	4.5641	.000
Nguyen (2012)	A	WDCT	Posttest	2.0893	.3497	.1223	1.4039	2.7747	5.9745	.000
Nguyen (2012)	B	WDCT	Posttest	.2818	.3087	.0953	−.3232	.8868	.9129	.361
Nguyen (2012)	C	Other	Posttest	2.6860	.3850	.1482	1.9314	3.4406	6.9765	.000
Nguyen (2012)	D	Other	Posttest	1.1614	.3375	.1139	.4999	1.8229	3.4413	.001
Nguyen (2012)	E	Other	Posttest	1.9376	.3381	.1143	1.2750	2.6003	5.7311	.000
Nguyen (2012)	F	Other	Posttest	.9507	.3291	.1083	.3056	1.5958	2.8884	.004
Nipaspong & Chinakoul (2008)	A	Other	Posttest	.4769	.3856	.1487	−.2788	1.2326	1.2370	.216
Nipaspong & Chinakoul (2008)	B	Other	Posttest	1.3206	.4217	.1778	.4941	2.1471	3.1318	.002
Niposponk & Chinoku (2010)	A	MDCT	Posttest	.3983	.3838	.1473	−.3540	1.1507	1.0378	.299
Niposponk & Chinoku (2010)	B	MDCT	Posttest	1.7109	.4479	.2006	.8331	2.5887	3.8202	.000
Omanee & Krishnasamy (2019)	M	WDCT	Posttest	2.2191	.3372	.1137	1.5582	2.8799	6.5813	.000
Omanee (2021)	A	WDCT	Posttest	1.7556	.3010	.0906	1.1655	2.3456	5.8315	.000
Omanee (2021)	B	WDCT	Posttest	.8275	.2658	.0707	.3065	1.3484	3.1131	.002

(continued)

(continued)

Study name	Subgroup	Outcome	Time point	Hedges' g	Std. error	Variance	Lower limit	Upper limit	Z-value	p-value
Pourmousavi & Mohamadi Zenouzagh (2020)	A	Other	Posttest	.9064	.2863	.0820	.3453	1.4676	3.1658	.002
Pourmousavi & Mohamadi Zenouzagh (2020)	B	Other	Posttest	.2840	.2425	.0588	−.1913	.7594	1.1711	.242
Rajabi, Azizifar & Gowhary (2015a)	A	WDCT	Posttest	2.3964	.4201	.1765	1.5731	3.2197	5.7048	.000
Rajabi, Azizifar & Gowhary (2015a)	B	WDCT	Posttest	2.8631	.4757	.2263	1.9307	3.7955	6.0185	.000
Rajabi, Azizifar & Gowhary (2015b)	A	WDCT	Posttest	1.4845	.3604	.1299	.7781	2.1909	4.1190	.000
Rajabi, Azizifar & Gowhary (2015b)	B	WDCT	Posttest	2.4454	.4412	.1946	1.5808	3.3101	5.5431	.000
Rajabi, Azizifar, & Gowhary (2015)	A	WDCT	Posttest	1.7332	.3481	.1212	1.0509	2.4155	4.9789	.000
Rajabi, Azizifar, & Gowhary (2015)	B	WDCT	Posttest	1.3070	.3133	.0981	.6930	1.9210	4.1720	.000
Razavi (2015)	M	WDCT	Posttest	1.9372	.3102	.0962	1.3293	2.5452	6.2452	.000
Rezvani, Eslami & Dastjerdi (2014)	A	WDCT	Posttest	1.8686	.2997	.0898	1.2812	2.4560	6.2352	.000
Rezvani, Eslami & Dastjerdi (2014)	B	WDCT	Posttest	1.9133	.3043	.0926	1.3167	2.5098	6.2865	.000
Saadatmandi. et al. (2018)	M	MDCT	Posttest	.5025	.2829	.0800	−.0520	1.0570	1.7762	.076
Sabzalipour & Koosha (2016)	A	MDCT	Posttest	1.1931	.2352	.0553	.7320	1.6542	5.0717	.000

(continued)

Appendix: Results for All Studies Included

(continued)

Study name	Subgroup	Outcome	Time point	Hedges' g	Std. error	Variance	Lower limit	Upper limit	Z-value	p-value
Sabzalipour & Koosha (2016)	B	MDCT	Posttest	.7951	.2650	.0702	.2758	1.3145	3.0007	.003
Sadeqi & Ghaemi (2016)	A	WDCT	Posttest	.8884	.3076	.0946	.2856	1.4913	2.8884	.004
Sadeqi & Ghaemi (2016)	B	MDCT	Posttest	.8556	.3066	.0940	.2547	1.4564	2.7910	.005
Salehi (2013)	M	WDCT	Posttest	.1916	.3107	.0965	-.4173	.8005	.6167	.537
Shirinbakhsh et al. (2016)	A	Other	Posttest	.5910	.2324	.0540	.1356	1.0465	2.5433	.011
Shirinbakhsh et al. (2016)	B	Other	Posttest	.7874	.2315	.0536	.3338	1.2411	3.4018	.001
Shirinbakhsh et al. (2016)	C	Other	Delayed	.7357	.2351	.0553	.2749	1.1965	3.1292	.002
Shirinbakhsh et al. (2016)	D	Other	Delayed	.7384	.2305	.0531	.2868	1.1901	3.2044	.001
Shirinbakhsh et al. (2016)	E	Other	Posttest	.0032	.2274	.0517	-.4425	.4489	.0139	.989
Shirinbakhsh et al. (2016)	F	Other	Posttest	.0009	.2228	.0497	-.4358	.4377	.0042	.997
Shirinbakhsh et al. (2016)	G	Other	Delayed	.5714	.2321	.0539	.1165	1.0262	2.4621	.014
Shirinbakhsh et al. (2016)	H	Other	Delayed	.0327	.2229	.0497	-.4041	.4694	.1466	.883
Soler & Pitarch (2010)	M	Other	Posttest	.0043	.1034	.0107	-.1984	.2069	.0413	.967
Taguchi & Tim (2014)	A	WDCT	Posttest	2.7989	.3988	.1590	2.0174	3.5805	7.0192	.000
Taguchi & Tim (2014)	B	WDCT	Posttest	1.8128	.3356	.1126	1.1551	2.4705	5.4023	.000
Taguchi & Tim (2014)	C	WDCT	Delayed	.2525	.2823	.0797	-.3008	.8059	.8945	.371
Taguchi & Tim (2014)	D	WDCT	Delayed	.4982	.2857	.0816	-.0617	1.0581	1.7441	.081
Taguchi & Tim (2014)	E	WDCT	Posttest	2.4598	.3752	.1408	1.7243	3.1952	6.5551	.000
Taguchi & Tim (2014)	F	WDCT	Posttest	3.2434	.4318	.1864	2.3972	4.0897	7.5122	.000
Taguchi & Tim (2014)	G	WDCT	Delayed	1.6674	.3278	.1074	1.0249	2.3098	5.0870	.000
Taguchi & Tim (2014)	H	WDCT	Delayed	1.7200	.3305	.1093	1.0722	2.3679	5.2037	.000

(continued)

(continued)

Study name	Subgroup	Outcome	Time point	Hedges' g	Std. error	Variance	Lower limit	Upper limit	Z-value	p-value
Taguchi & Tim (2014)	I	WDCT	Posttest	.1326	.2815	.0792	−.4192	.6843	.4710	.638
Taguchi & Tim (2014)	J	WDCT	Posttest	.1922	.2819	.0794	−.3602	.7447	.6820	.495
Taguchi & Tim (2014)	K	WDCT	Delayed	.2927	.2827	.0799	−.2615	.8468	1.0352	.301
Taguchi & Tim (2014)	L	WDCT	Delayed	.5354	.2863	.0820	−.0259	1.0966	1.8697	.062
Taguchi & Tim (2014)	N	WDCT	Posttest	1.5525	.3220	.1037	.9215	2.1836	4.8220	.000
Taguchi & Tim (2014)	O	WDCT	Posttest	1.2600	.3087	.0953	.6550	1.8649	4.0821	.000
Taguchi & Tim (2014)	P	WDCT	Delayed	.0835	.2813	.0791	−.4679	.6349	.2968	.767
Taguchi & Tim (2014)	Q	WDCT	Delayed	.2706	.2825	.0798	−.2831	.8243	.9579	.338
Taguchi & Tim (2014)	R	WDCT	Posttest	.1907	.2818	.0794	−.3617	.7431	.6766	.499
Taguchi & Tim (2014)	S	WDCT	Posttest	.5071	.2858	.0817	−.0531	1.0673	1.7741	.076
Taguchi & Tim (2014)	T	WDCT	Delayed	.0749	.2813	.0791	−.4764	.6262	.2662	.790
Taguchi & Tim (2014)	U	WDCT	Delayed	.1415	.2816	.0793	−.4104	.6933	.5024	.615
Tajeddin & Bagherkazemi (2014)	A	WDCT	Posttest	4.6057	.4630	.2144	3.6982	5.5133	9.9466	.000
Tajeddin & Bagherkazemi (2014)	B	WDCT	Delayed	4.9355	.4935	.2435	3.9683	5.9028	10.0010	.000
Tajeddin & Bagherkazemi (2014)	C	WDCT	Delayed	1.3582	.1873	.0351	.9912	1.7253	7.2521	.000
Tajeddin et al. (2012)	A	WDCT	Posttest	1.8515	.3137	.0984	1.2367	2.4662	5.9025	.000
Tajeddin et al. (2012)	B	WDCT	Posttest	1.8326	.3174	.1007	1.2105	2.4547	5.7735	.000
Tajjedin & Hosseinpur (2014a)	A	WDCT	Posttest	.2993	.1483	.0220	.0087	.5899	2.0183	.044

(continued)

(continued)

Study name	Subgroup	Outcome	Time point	Hedges' g	Std. error	Variance	Lower limit	Upper limit	Z-value	p-value
Tajjedin & Hosseinpur (2014a)	B	WDCT	Posttest	.2670	.1461	.0213	−.0193	.5534	1.8277	.068
Tajjedin & Hosseinpur (2014a)	C	WDCT	Posttest	.3874	.1489	.0222	.0955	.6793	2.6010	.009
Tajjedin & Hosseinpur (2014b)	A	WDCT	Posttest	.2428	.0853	.0073	.0756	.4100	2.8468	.004
Tajjedin & Hosseinpur (2014b)	B	WDCT	Delayed	.5044	.0893	.0080	.3293	.6794	5.6479	.000
Tajjedin & Hosseinpur (2014b)	C	WDCT	Post Delayed	.1392	.0845	.0071	−.0263	.3048	1.6482	.099
Tanak & Oki (2015)	M	Other	Posttest	.4306	.1664	.0277	.1045	.7568	2.5878	.010
Usó-Juan (2022)	M	Other	Posttest	2.4561	.2516	.0633	1.9631	2.9492	9.7638	.000
Xiao-Le (2011)	A	WDCT	Posttest	.1382	.0647	.0042	.0115	.2649	2.1379	.033
Xiao-Le (2011)	B	WDCT	Posttest	3.7961	.1848	.0342	3.4338	4.1583	20.5383	.000
Zand-Moghadam & Samani (2021)	A	WDCT	Posttest	3.7158	.6255	.3913	2.4898	4.9418	5.9405	.000
Zand-Moghadam & Samani (2021)	B	WDCT	Posttest	3.2221	.5528	.3056	2.1385	4.3056	5.8283	.000
Zand-Moghadam & Samani (2021)	C	WDCT	Posttest	2.7606	.4864	.2366	1.8072	3.7139	5.6753	.000
Zanguie et al. (2014)	M	MDCT	Posttest	.8633	.2585	.0668	.3567	1.3700	3.3400	.001
Ziafar (2018)	A	MDCT	Posttest	1.4359	.3052	.0932	.8377	2.0342	4.7045	.000
Ziafar (2018)	B	MDCT	Posttest	1.2761	.2815	.0792	.7244	1.8278	4.5334	.000
Ziafar (2018)	C	MDCT	Posttest	1.5520	.3260	.1063	.9130	2.1910	4.7603	.000

(continued)

(continued)

Study name	Subgroup	Outcome	Time point	Hedges' g	Std. error	Variance	Lower limit	Upper limit	Z-value	p-value
Ziashahabi et al. (2020)	A	MDCT	Posttest	1.9867	.3724	.1387	1.2569	2.7166	5.3352	.000
Ziashahabi et al. (2020)	B	MDCT	Posttest	.8738	.3174	.1008	.2516	1.4960	2.7526	.006
Ziashahabi et al. (2020)	C	MDCT	Delayed	2.1170	.3808	.1450	1.3706	2.8634	5.5589	.000
Ziashahabi et al. (2020)	D	MDCT	Delayed	1.0716	.3246	.1053	.4354	1.7077	3.3015	.001
Fixed Effect				.9964	.0179	.0003	.9613	1.0314	55.6574	.000
Random Effect				1.6968	.0726	.0053	1.5545	1.8392	23.3682	.000